ROCKS & FOSSILS

VISUAL FACTFINDER

ROCKS & FOSSILS

Written by: Chris and Helen Pellant
Consulted by: Steve Parker

Miles
Kelly
PUBLISHING

First published in 2007 by Miles Kelly Publishing Ltd
Bardfield Centre, Great Bardfield, Essex, CM7 4SL

2 4 6 8 10 9 7 5 3 1

Editorial Director Belinda Gallagher
Art Director Jo Brewer
Assistant Editor Lucy Dowling
Designer Candice Bekir
Picture Researcher Laura Faulder
Production Manager Elizabeth Brunwin
Reprographics Anthony Cambray,
Stephan Davis, Liberty Newton, Ian Paulyn
Indexers Mary Orchard at The Indexing
Specialists (UK) Ltd, Jane Parker

British Library Cataloguing-in-Publication Data
A catalogue record for this book is available from the British Library

ISBN: 978-1-84236-901-2

Printed in China

www.mileskelly.net
info@mileskelly.net

ROCKS AND MINERALS 14–281

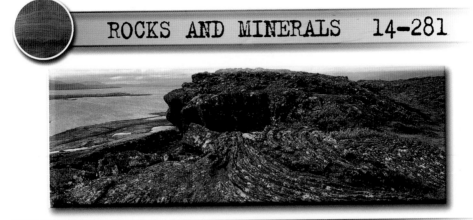

IGNEOUS ROCKS UNDERGROUND

IGNEOUS ROCKS ON THE SURFACE

SEDIMENTARY ROCKS

METAMORPHIC ROCKS

ALL ABOUT MINERALS

MINERALS, GEMS AND THEIR USES

FOSSILS 282-483

GRAPTOLITES AND ARTHROPODS

MOLLUSCS

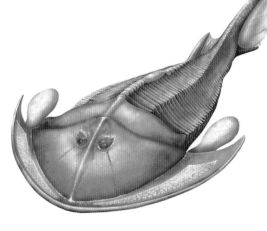

VERTEBRATES

DINOSAURS

MAMMALS

What is a rock?

- **A rock is an aggregate** (mixture) of mineral particles. It may be made of loose sand (sandstone) or sticky clay (mudstone), fossil and fossil debris (limestone) or mineral crystals welded together (igneous and high grade metamorphic rocks).

- **Scientists classify rocks** into three main groups – igneous, sedimentary and metamorphic.

- **Rocks began to form** as soon as the original molten (liquid) Earth started to cool around 4000 million years ago.

- **The first rocks to form** were igneous rocks. These crystallized from molten magma (underground) or lava (on the surface).

- **Rocks form in a cycle.** Igneous rocks are weathered and eroded and formed into sedimentary rocks. These may be altered by metamorphism (the effect of extreme heat or pressure) and eventually, if they are buried very deep in the Earth's crust, they melt and become igneous rocks again.

- **The age of rocks** can be worked out by studying the fossils they contain or the breakdown of radio-active elements contained in them. This is called radiometric dating.

- **As soon as the Earth's atmosphere** had begun to develop, around 2000 million years ago, weathering and erosion began to break down the early igneous rocks to make sediments.

....FASCINATING FACT....
The oldest rocks to be radiometrically dated are over 3900 million years old.

- **Metamorphic rocks** are created when earlier-formed rocks are changed by heat from magma or lava or by pressure and heat deep underground.

- **Rocks are being formed** all the time. The mud and sand on the beach or in a riverbed may become a sedimentary rock.

◀ *This cliff face shows layers of sedimentary sandstone at the top. Below these there is a narrow layer of very pale metamorphic rock and at the bottom an uneven mass of igneous dolerite.*

15

What are igneous rocks?

- **Geologists** sometimes call igneous rocks primary rocks because they form from molten material that originates deep in the Earth's crust.

- **Igneous rocks** can be distinguished from other rocks because they are made of a mosaic of mineral crystals, usually without layers.

- **The crystals** in igneous rocks are usually welded together.

- **Igneous rocks** occur in many different structures, both underground (intrusive) and on the surface (extrusive).

- **Intrusive** igneous rocks form underground in large masses called batholiths, and relatively small intrusions, for example, sills and dykes.

- **Extrusive** igneous rocks build volcanoes. These may have large rocky craters or be mountains of ash and dust.

◀ *In a thin slice of granite magnified many times, the crystals are clearly seen. The grey crystals are quartz and feldspar and the brighter colours are mica.*

- **Igneous rocks** are the best rocks for radiometric dating because the crystals in them formed at a definite time in the past. These crystals may not have altered since their formation, so an accurate date can often be obtained. Radiometric dating is most accurate if the rocks used are fresh and unweathered.

- **Basalt** is a volcanic igneous rock that makes up more of the Earth's crust than any other rock. It covers the vast ocean basins.

- **Granite**, an intrusive igneous rock that forms deep underground, makes up much of the Earth's continental crust.

- **Some igneous rocks**, such as granite and dolerite, are very hard and durable and are quarried for use in road surfaces.

▼ *Crater Lake in Oregon, USA is the remains of a collapsed volcano called a caldera. The small cone forms Wizard Island.*

How igneous rocks vary

- **Igneous rocks** differ from each other in two main ways – what they are made of and the size of their crystals.

- **The composition** of an igneous rock is not usually complex, and consists of very few minerals.

- **One main group** of igneous rocks, which geologists call felsic (acid) rocks, is made largely of three easily identified minerals – quartz, feldspar and mica.

▼ *Lava can erupt in a violent, frothy mass, containing a lot of gas. When it cools, it is full of gas-bubble holes.*

▶ *These brightly coloured lumps of lava, each a few centimetres across, are called rainbow slag. This volcanic rock occurs in southern Iceland.*

- **Acid rocks** are usually pale-coloured and not very heavy.

- **Another important group** is made of feldspar, olivine and pyroxene, with only a small amount of quartz. These are called mafic (basic) rocks.

- **Basic rocks** are generally dark-coloured and heavier than you'd expect when picked up.

- **If an igneous rock** solidifies as magma cools deep underground, the crystals it is made of will often be large enough to see with the naked eye. Geologists refer to these rocks as coarse-grained.

- **Igneous rocks** that solidify as lava cools on the Earth's surface have very small mineral crystals. A microscope may be required to see them. These rocks are fine-grained.

- **Sometimes magma** or lava cools in two stages – one deep underground and the other on, or near, the surface. If this happens, the rock will contain some large crystals and some smaller ones.

- **Volcanic rocks** include a whole range of fragments blown to bits by an eruption. Examples are dust, ash and pumice.

19

Granite

▲ *This granite on the Isle of Mull, western Scotland, has been weathered along its vertical joints. The pink colour results from large amounts of feldspar in the rock.*

- **Granite** is one of the best-known igneous rocks because of its colourful crystalline appearance. Polished slabs are used to decorate buildings.

- **It is a coarse-grained** igneous rock with crystals that are easily seen by the naked eye. They are generally more than 5 mm across. Granite also contains white or pink crystals of feldspar and black or silvery white mica.

- **Other minerals** found in granite, which don't affect its classification, are called accessory minerals. These include pyrite, tourmaline and apatite.

- **Granite contains** a large amount of quartz. This common mineral is off white or grey, greasy-looking and very hard.

- **Granite forms** deep in the Earth's crust in large chambers of molten magma called batholiths. The magma cools very slowly, often taking many millions of years, which enables the crystals in granite to grow to a large size.

- **For granite to be exposed** at the surface, many thousands of metres of rock have to be weathered and eroded. Rocks may also be pushed up by mountain building processes before granite is exposed on the Earth's surface.

- **Granite** is not as hard and durable as many people think. It is easily weathered, especially in humid climates, and decomposes to sand and clay.

- **In the area around** a mass of granite, there is a region of metamorphism where heat from the magma has changed the original rocks.

- **In the area** near to a granite batholith it may be possible to mine for tin, copper, lead, zinc and other minerals.

Batholiths

- **A batholith** is a very large mass of igneous rock that was originally magma.

- **Batholiths** are commonly formed deep in the roots of mountain chains and may be many tens of kilometres in diameter.

- **In Britain**, a batholith exists under much of Cornwall and reaches out under the sea to the Scilly Isles. This covers an area of 65 km by 40 km. Many batholiths are larger than this.

- **Before the giant mass** of magma in the batholith was intruded (forced in), there was other rock in that part of the Earth's crust. Geologists have puzzled over what happened to the original rock. It is believed that some of it was melted and incorporated into the magma.

- **Granite magma** itself may be the result of the melting of other rock at great depth.

- **Sills and dykes** may stretch upwards from some batholiths.

- **Most batholiths** are made of granite. Some contain other coarse-grained igneous rocks like syenite and gabbro.

- **Even when the rock** in a batholith has been crystalline for millions of years, heat will still rise through it from a great depth. This heat may be trapped if clay and other rock have formed later.

- **Scientists** have discovered that this heat could be used to produce electricity in a safe, clean way.

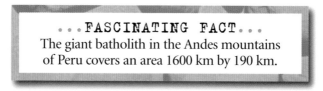

... FASCINATING FACT ...
The giant batholith in the Andes mountains
of Peru covers an area 1600 km by 190 km.

▼ *A batholith is a gigantic mass of magma formed deep below a mountain range. Small offshoots of magma may rise from it higher into the Earth's crust. Lumps of rock called xenoliths may be present in the batholith.*

Batholith

Xenolith

Granodiorite

- **One of the most common** igneous rocks is granodiorite.

- **As its name suggests,** this rock has some features of the acidic granites and some features of the intermediate rocks.

- **Granodiorite is an attractive,** coarse-grained rock. The crystals making up the mass of the rock can easily be seen with the naked eye.

▼ *This attractive rock is coloured by its minerals. The pink mineral is feldspar, dark colours are hornblende and biotite mica, and the pale mineral is quartz.*

- **The main minerals** in granodiorite are feldspar, quartz, hornblende, augite and mica.

- **There are two main colour varieties** of granodiorite. One is pink because of the colour of most of the feldspar in the rock. White granodiorite contains pale–coloured feldspar.

- **This rock looks** similar to granite. When its minerals are examined and the total silica content worked out, it can be seen that it is an intermediate, not an acid rock.

- **In many types of igneous intrusions,** granodiorite can be found, especially those formed at some depth below the Earth's surface.

- **When this rock occurs** in large intrusions, it is often associated with granite.

- **The vast batholith** in southern California covers a surface area of more than 7700 sq km. Much of it is made of granodiorite.

- **Because of its colouring** and crystalline appearance, granodiorite is used for ornamental purposes.

. . . .FASCINATING FACT. . . .
Much of the so-called 'granite' used as a
decorative polished rock is actually granodiorite.

Gabbro

- **Gabbro** is a dark igneous rock. It is made of quite large crystals and has a speckled appearance.

- **Gabbro** forms as large masses of magma cool, as granite does, but it is made of different minerals. Because it cools slowly, it has large, easily visible crystals.

- **Rather than occurring** in batholiths, gabbro is commonly found in thick sheets of igneous rock.

- **Feldpsar and pyroxene** are the two main minerals in gabbro, but it also has a small amount of quartz – less than 10 percent.

- **Feldspar is a pale mineral**, often occurring in thin crystals in gabbro, while pyroxene is almost black, giving the rock its speckled appearance.

- **Compared with granite**, gabbro is a very dark-coloured rock, and is also noticeably heavier. This is because it contains a large amount of pyroxene, which is a dense mineral.

- **A mineral called olivine** is sometimes found in gabbro. This is a green or brownish mineral rich in iron and magnesium, which crystallizes at very high temperatures.

- **Gabbro** mainly forms in the Earth's crust beneath the basalts of the ocean floors but can also occur on continents. Granite typically occurs in a continental setting.

- **Some famous masses** of gabbro are at Bushveldt in South Africa and Stillwater, Montana, USA.

- **In Britain**, the Cuillin Hills on the Isle of Skye, in western Scotland are largely made of gabbro, which weathers into jagged peaks.

Gabbro

▲ *The jagged gabbro peaks of the Cuillins seen across Loch Slapin on the Isle of Skye.*

Pegmatite

▲ *This intrusion of pegmatite is full of large, pink feldspar crystals. It has cut into dark-coloured metamorphic rock.*

● **Pegmatite** is an igneous rock formed deep underground and made up of very large crystals. These may be over 3 cm long. In some pegmatite rocks, giant crystals over one metre long have been discovered.

- **For such large crystals to form**, the magma must cool very slowly, allowing the crystals a long time to develop.

- **Pegmatite** occurs in sheets and other structures, often around the margins of large scale intrusions.

- **Sills and dykes** of pegmatite also occur in many areas of very old gneiss.

- **Usually**, pegmatite has a similar composition to granite, containing mainly feldspar, mica and quartz. However, gabbro and syenite pegmatites are not unknown.

- **Pegmatite** generally crystallizes from magma and other high-temperature fluids, which are rich in many rare elements. These include niobium, tantalum, lithium and tungsten. This makes some pegmatites economically valuable.

- **Among the extra minerals** that are often found in pegmatites are tourmaline, topaz, fluorite, apatite and cassiterite.

- **Radioactive elements**, such as autunite and torbernite, also occur in pegmatite.

- **Some pegmatites** have an attractive appearance called graphic texture. This looks rather like ancient writing and is created by quartz and feldspar crystals merging in the rock.

> ...FASCINATING FACT...
> A crystal of the mineral beryl, nearly 6 m long, and a spodumene crystal over 15 m long, were found in a pegmatite in South Dakota, USA.

Porphyry

- **Rocks of medium grain size** that contain large crystals set into the finer ground mass are referred to as porphyry.

- **These rocks have formed** in minor intrusions, such as sills and dykes.

- **The word porphyry** comes from the Greek *porphyra*, meaning purple. The renowned Imperial Porphyry, which was extinsively used in ancient Greece, was a purplish stone for decoration.

- **Porphyry is still used** as an ornamental stone today.

- **The name porphyry** is often used in combination with a mineral name, such as quartz porphyry.

- **The large crystals in porphyry** are usually feldspars, but may be quartz, or other minerals.

- **The formation of porphyry** is closely related to the way in which magma, from which the rock is made, has cooled.

- **Molten rock found deep in the Earth's crust** is called magma. When it rises, it cools, and minerals then crystallize. The magma around the first crystals to form is still liquid and mobile.

- **Magma containing solid crystals** may rise into a fracture in the crust and form a dyke. The mass of rock will cool rapidly around the previously formed crystals, making porphyry.

- **A very striking form** of porphyry, which comes from Scandinavia, contains large, diamond-shaped crystals, and is called rhomb porphyry.

▶ *Large feldspar and other crystals set in a fine-grained, dark matrix give this andesite, from Scandinavia, a porphyritic texture.*

Xenolith

- **The word 'xenolith'** comes from the Greek *xenos*, which means 'stranger' and *lithos*, meaning 'stone'.

- **These 'stranger stones'** are found around the margins of many igneous intrusions, where magma has melted and forced its way into other rocks. They may also be found in lava.

- **They are lumps of rock** that have been broken off and engulfed by the igneous rock, so are strangers in their new location.

- **Xenoliths** often appear as dark, rounded or irregular rocks set into granite or another igneous rock.

- **Near the very edge** of the igneous intrusion, a xenolith will not have been heated too much by the magma and so keeps many of its original features.

- **Xenoliths** found some metres into the igneous rock will have been altered considerably and metamorphosed. They may even have crystals in them similar to those in the igneous rock.

- **Xenoliths** help geologists to work out the types of rock the magma passed through, as it was being intruded or erupted.

- **In some places** blocks of the very lowest crustal rocks have been brought to the surface by rising magma. These xenoliths allow geologists to study rocks not normally seen on the surface.

- **In the diamond-bearing rocks** around Kimberly, South Africa, xenoliths that may be derived from the Earth's mantle (the region beneath the crust) are found.

- **Large amounts of xenolith rock** caught up in magma may react with it and change its composition.

▼ *Large, dark xenoliths can be easily seen in this eroded mass of igneous diorite. They were surrounded by molten magma and partly changed by its heat.*

Syenite

▼ Syenite has large crystals because it formed as magma cooled slowly. The pale crystals are feldspar and the darker patches are made of mica, pyroxene and hornblende.

- **Syenite** is an intrusive igneous rock that has formed by the cooling of magma deep in the Earth's crust.

- **Because of the slow cooling** associated with the high temperatures at great depth, syenite has large crystals and is a coarse-grained rock. The crystals can be seen with the naked eye.

- **Syenite** may look rather like granite, but by studying the minerals it contains, differences can be seen.

- **Syenite** will usually appear darker-coloured than granite, but not as dark as gabbro. Some syenites may be pink or grey or tinged with violet.

- **One well-known** type of syenite is called larvikite. It is from Norway and is commonly cut into slabs and polished to make a pearly blue-green ornamental stone. This has been used as a facing stone on many buildings throughout the UK.

- **As well as occurring** in large intrusions, syenite is also found in sills and dykes. These rocks tend to have smaller crystals.

- **Many syenites** have large crystals set into a finer mass, giving an attractive appearance. This is called a porphyritic texture.

- **As well as feldspar and quartz,** syenite can contain hornblende, pyroxene and the dark mica biotite. This composition contains features of both granite and gabbro.

- **Microsyenite** is an igneous rock with the composition of syenite but contains smaller crystals.

- **Rhomb porphyry** is a type of microsyenite found commonly in Norway. Pebbles of it, which have been carried by ice sheets across the North Sea area, are often found on the east coast of England.

Larvikite

- **Syenite that is found** mainly around Oslo in Norway is called larvikite.

- **The rock is named** after the town of Larvik, south of Oslo.

- **Larvikite is a coarse-grained rock** and the large crystals can easily be seen with the naked eye.

- **Larvikite is one of the most attractive** igneous rocks, especially when cut and polished.

- **It is extensively used** on the front of buildings, as well as for smaller scale decorative purposes, such as kitchen work surfaces.

- **This rock is dark coloured** and prized for its bluish iridescence, which is called schillerization.

- **The schillerization is caused** by the large, distinctive feldspars in the rock, and is best seen on polished surfaces.

- **As a syenite**, larvikite has an intermediate composition. It contains mainly feldspar, along with augite, mica, olivine, hornblende and rarely quartz.

- **It occurs in igneous intrusions** such as sills, which were formed at a depth of 3–4 kilometres. These are called concordant intrusions, as they follow existing rock structures.

...**FASCINATING FACT**...
Larvikite is often referred to as 'blue granite' when used ornamentally. This name has no geological meaning. Larvikite is a form of syenite, not of granite.

▶ *When polished for ornamental use, the bluish iridescence of the feldspar crystals in larvikite can easily be seen.*

Dykes and sills

- **Dykes and sills** are called minor igneous intrusions because they are of moderate to small size.

- **Both intrusions** are sheets of igneous rock and are commonly made of rocks such as dolerite that have cooled quite quickly and are fine grained.

- **They are** usually measured in metres, being anything from one or two metres in thickness to a few hundred.

- **A dyke** is very often a vertical sheet of dark rock cutting across existing strata (layers). Geologists call this a discordant intrusion.

- **The magma** forming the dyke will have risen into a fracture in the overlying rocks.

- **Dykes are often found** in great numbers, or swarms. One such swarm occurs in the Inner Hebrides across southern Scotland and stretches into the north of England.

- **A sill**, in contrast, follows the rock structures in the area where it is intruded. This is called a concordant intrusion. In sedimentary rocks, they are generally intruded along bedding planes.

- **Because they are small** structures giving out little heat, there is usually only a small metamorphic effect on neighbouring rocks.

- **Like many lava flows**, sills may form vertical columns of rock that results from the way the magma has cooled. This is known as columnar jointing.

> **...FASCINATING FACT...**
> On the Isle of Arran, Scotland, 525 dykes occur within a distance of 24 km. These have stretched the Earth's crust by 7 percent.

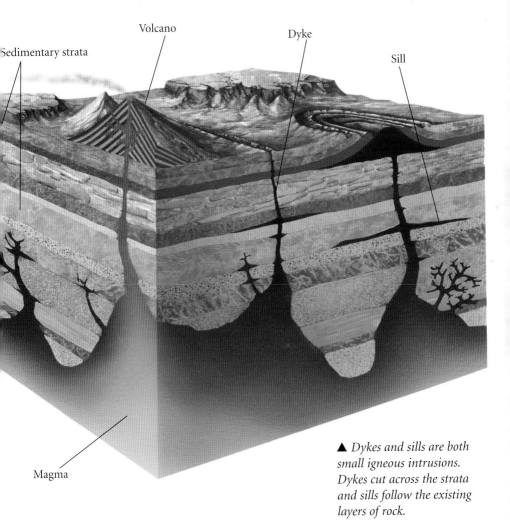

Volcano

Dyke

Sedimentary strata

Sill

Magma

▲ *Dykes and sills are both small igneous intrusions. Dykes cut across the strata and sills follow the existing layers of rock.*

Dolerite

- **Dolerite** is a dark-coloured igneous rock, often with an overall speckled appearance.

- **The speckled surface** results from the minerals it contains. These are light-coloured feldspar and black pyroxene. There is also a small amount of pale grey quartz. This is the same composition as gabbro and basalt.

- **Dolerite** may contain the green or brownish mineral called olivine.

- **It is possible** to see its crystals with the naked eye, but to study them in detail a strong hand lens is needed. Geologists refer to this type of rock as being medium-grained.

- **Dolerite** commonly occurs in small igneous intrusions, such as sills and dykes, where magma has cooled much more rapidly than in a batholith.

- **Rounded vertical masses** of dolerite may be the necks of old volcanoes. These remain after the lava and ash of the volcano have been eroded.

- **Dolerite-forming magma** originates very low in the Earth's crust or in the upper mantle. The rock is generally associated with thin oceanic crust rather than areas of thick continental crust.

- **Dolerite** is a dense, heavy rock mainly because it contains minerals that are rich in iron.

- **American geologists** use the term diabase for this type of rock.

- **Dolerite** is a very hard and durable rock. It is extensively quarried for road stone, railway ballast and other uses.

◄ *Because dolerite forms from magma that has cooled relatively quickly, its crystals are not easy to see. A powerful hand lens would be needed to see the crystals in detail.*

Serpentinite

- **Serpentinite** is unlike many igneous rocks in a number of vital ways. It is thought to be formed by the chemical alteration of other igneous rocks.

- **It often contains** very attractive colours, such as shades of green and red. These colours often make veins through the rock.

- **Because it is easily cut**, shaped and polished, serpentinite is often used ornamentally. This is especially true in areas where it is a common rock, such as around the Lizard peninsula in Cornwall, UK.

- **Serpentinite** is made largely of a variety of 'serpentine' minerals. These include chrysotile and antigorite, which are both silicate minerals with a slippery, soapy feel and fibrous structure.

- **Chrysotile** is a source of asbestos, once used for its insulating properties.

- **Serpentinites** contain virtually no quartz, but can contain a number of silicate minerals, such as garnet, mica, hornblende and pyroxene.

- **It is generally believed** that serpentinites were originally dense, heavy rocks related to the lowest parts of the Earth's crust. These were rich in minerals such as olivine, and have been much altered by the addition of water.

- **In some examples**, there is little indication as to what the original rock may have been because the serpentinization is so extreme.

- **Serpentinites** are found in many areas, including Cornwall, Anglesey and Shetland, UK; New Zealand; New South Wales, Australia, and Montana, USA.

- **Serpentine minerals** are also found in a group of meteorites called carbonaceous chondrites.

▼ *The coast of the Lizard Peninsula in Cornwall, UK, where serpentinite occurs.*

Volcanoes

- **A volcano** is an opening in the Earth's crust through which lava escapes.

- **Depending on the type** of lava and other volcanic materials, the volcano may be a low, gently sloping structure or a steep, cone-shaped mountain.

- **Some volcanoes** have a single opening. These are called central volcanoes. Others have a number of vents and are called fissure volcanoes.

- **Volcanoes** from which basalt lava erupts are not as violent as those that produce rhyolite and andesite lavas. Basaltic lava has a higher temperature and a less sticky silica than rhyolite and andesite lavas. This means that it flows easily away from the vent.

- **The Hawaiian**, or shield, volcanoes are made of basalt. They have large craters and low domes that spread many tens of kilometres. The base of Mauna Loa in Hawaii is 112 km in diameter.

- **Strombolian volcanoes**, named after the island of Stromboli to the north of Sicily, are classic cone shapes. Eruptions can be violent. As well as lava there are layers of ash and dust.

- **Vesuvian volcanoes**, named after Mt Vesuvius in Italy, erupt only once every ten or more years. The lava is sticky and plugs the vent, causing violent eruptions.

- **Pelean volcanoes**, named after Mt Pelee in Martinique, are amongst the most violent. These erupt sticky, silica-rich lava, which often solidifies in the volcano. A great pressure then builds up as more lava tries to get through, and much of the volcano is blown apart by the eruption.

- **Volcanoes** can be very destructive. In 1883, Krakatoa in Java erupted, sending a huge dust cloud around the Earth's atmosphere. This affected the climate for three years. Over 36,000 people died as a result of the eruption.

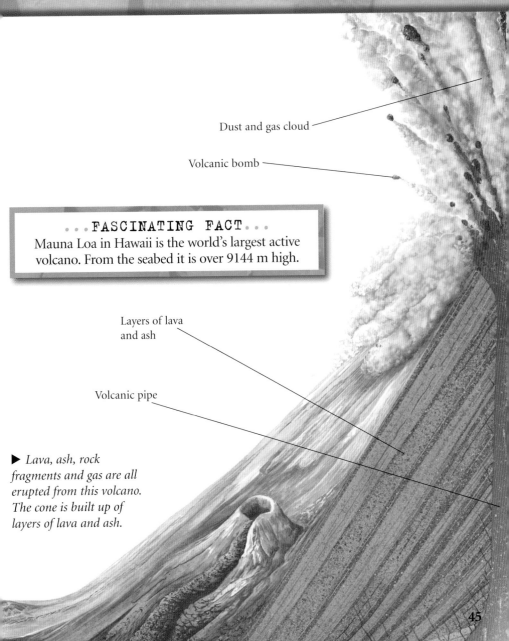

Dust and gas cloud

Volcanic bomb

> ...FASCINATING FACT...
> Mauna Loa in Hawaii is the world's largest active
> volcano. From the seabed it is over 9144 m high.

Layers of lava
and ash

Volcanic pipe

▶ *Lava, ash, rock
fragments and gas are all
erupted from this volcano.
The cone is built up of
layers of lava and ash.*

45

Where volcanoes occur

- **The distribution of volcanoes** is closely linked to lines of weakness in the Earth's crust and its varying thickness.

- **In ocean areas**, the crust is less than 10 km thick, but below the great continents it may be 60 km thick. Lava can more easily escape to the surface where the crust is thin.

▼ *On the deep ocean bed where slabs of the Earth's crust move apart, lava erupts to form a range of underwater volcanic mountains.*

Ridges are low and older away from centre

Sea level

Mid-ocean ridge

Central canyon

Transform fault

Ocean plate

- **The Earth's crust** and the uppermost part of the underlying layer, the mantle, make up the lithosphere. This is divided into a number of plates.

- **The lithospheric plates** are internally solid but constantly move. Some collide, others move away from each other. It is along these plate boundaries that volcanic activity is concentrated.

- **The 'Ring of Fire'** around the Pacific Ocean has been studied for many years as many of the world's volcanoes are located in this region. The Pacific Ocean floor is the largest of Earth's plates and around its edges are weaknesses where erupting basaltic lavas can well up to the surface.

- **The volcanoes** in Southeast Asia, Japan, South and North America are all part of the Ring of Fire.

- **In the Atlantic,** the situation is different. There are two major plates making up this ocean basin, which are moving away from each other. The Mid-Atlantic Ridge, which is mainly below sea level, is a line of active volcanoes.

- **In Iceland,** the Mid-Atlantic Ridge reaches above sea level. This large island is made almost entirely of volcanic rock.

- **There are other regions** where eruptions are caused by plates moving apart from each other. The African Rift Valley is one place where this process is beginning – volcanoes such as Kilimanjaro occur.

- **The Hawaiian volcanoes** are in the centre of the Pacific plate, forming a chain of islands. They lie above a plume of hot material rising from the base of the crust.

Basalt

- **Basalt** makes up more of the Earth's crust than any other rock. Beneath a thin layer of sediment, it covers the ocean floor. More than 90 percent of the volcanic rocks found on the Earth are basalt.

- **Basalt** is a volcanic rock that often erupts non-violently and can flow great distances.

- **It is a dark-coloured rock** and its crystals can rarely be seen on its surface without a microscope. Basalt is what geologists call a fine-grained rock.

- **The composition** of basalt is the same as that of gabbro and dolerite. It contains small crystals of feldspar, pyroxene and common olivine with a small amount of quartz.

- **When it erupts**, basalt lava contains much gas. As the rock cools, gas-bubble hollows are left in the solid rock. These are called vesicles, and give the rock a rough texture.

- **Many fine mineral specimens**, including agate, develop in the vesicles, often long after the rock has cooled.

- **Basalt** is a dense, heavy rock. It contains iron-rich minerals, which because of their magnetism, have been of great use in working out the movement of the Earth's plates.

- **Basalt lava flows** often develop amazingly regular six-sided columns when cool. The Giant's Causeway in Northern Ireland is a fine example of this feature.

- **Rocks recovered** from the Moon are basaltic. These contain very similar minerals to those found in terrestrial basalts.

▶ *The flow lines can be clearly seen on the surface of this basalt in Iceland.*

Andesite

- **The rock andesite** is solidified from a type of lava that erupts from violent volcanoes.

- **The name of this rock** is taken from the Andes mountains in South America, where much of the rock occurs.

- **Andesite is a fine-grained rock.** The individual crystals making the body of the rock (its matrix) cannot be seen in detail with the naked eye.

- **This type of lava** is referred to by geologists as an intermediate igneous rock. It is between basalt and rhyolite in its chemical composition.

- **The main minerals** in andesite are plagioclase feldspar, pyroxene, amphibole, biotite and mica.

- **This rock has a medium** to dark colour. It is not as dark as basalt, nor as pale in colour as rhyolite.

- **Some andesite lavas** are so rich in gas that when they solidify into rock, the rock is filled with gas cavities called vesicles.

- **Large crystals, a few centimetres in length**, occur in some andesites. These formed before the lava erupted. Such rocks are said to have a porphyritic texture.

...FASCINATING FACT...
Andesite volcanoes erupt large amounts of dust and ash. The devastating eruption of Krakatoa in 1883 produced millions of tonnes of andesite lava. Its eruption could be heard nearly 5000 km away.

▼ *The crater of Poas, Costa Rica, is filled with a pool of highly acidic water. Layers of andesitic ash and lava can be seen around the crater rim.*

Rhyolite

- **This hard, flinty rock** is formed by the solidifying of lava.

- **This rock contains** a high proportion of silica, which means the lava from which rhyolite forms is classified by geologists as acidic lava.

- **As acid lavas** contain more than 65 percent silica they are viscous (sticky).

- **The volcanoes from which rhyolitic lava** is erupted are extremely violent. This is because the viscous lava doesn't flow far, and may block the vent as it cools, leading to a build-up of pressure.

- **Some acidic lava volcanoes** develop a tall spine of solidified rhyolite lava above the cone.

▼ *Rhyolite volcanoes are explosive and very violent when they erupt.*

▶ *The thin lines in this close-up specimen of rhyolite are called flow-banding. They were caused when molten lava flowed from the volcano.*

● **Rhyolite is generally a pale coloured rock**, paler than basalt or andesite.

● **The minerals in rhyolite** are too small to be seen without a hand lens or microscope. This is because it has solidified quickly.

● **Rhyolite contains high proportions** of quartz and feldspar. These minerals are often glassy, as they have cooled so rapidly. Mica may also occur.

● **A banded structure**, often seen in rhyolite, results from the flow of the molten rock.

. . .FASCINATING FACT. . .

Because it is hard, and may break with a sharp fracture, rhyolite was used for making tools and axes during Neolithic times.

Obsidian

▼ *Obsidian is formed from lava that cools so fast that it turns into glass. The white spots in this snowflake obsidian are where the glass has been altered.*

- **When lava erupts** rapidly onto the Earth's surface, it is suddenly in an environment a thousand degrees cooler than the one it was in underground.

- **Such a rapid temperature** change causes the lava to freeze and solidify rapidly. The rock formed may have a glassy surface with no crystals visible.

- **Obsidian** is a rock that is formed under these conditions, and it contains no real crystals.

- **With the help** of microscopes and chemical analysis, geologists have found that obsidian is related to granite in composition and to another volcanic rock called rhyolite.

- **Pitchstone** is a rock that is rather like obsidian, but contains more crystalline material and its surface is more like pitch, or tar.

- **When broken**, obsidian has a very sharp, curved surface. This is called a conchoidal (shell-like) fracture.

- **Its sharp fracture** has been exploited by primitive people for making weapons and other implements, as it can be easily and accurately shaped.

- **Snowflake obsidian** is an attractive rock covered with small white patches. These occur where the volcanic glass has deteriorated. This rock is often cut and polished.

- **Obsidian is a well-known rock**, but is not very common. Hecla in Iceland and Obsidian Cliff in Yellowstone National Park, USA are famous locations.

...FASCINATING FACT...
The most striking feature of obsidian is
that it looks just like a piece of black glass.

Tuff and bomb

- **As well as lava**, volcanoes erupt other material. Most of this is broken rock, dust, ash and volcanic bombs.

- **Ash and dust** from a volcano may be thrown high into the atmosphere. Much of this material, especially the larger fragments, falls near the volcano.

- **When it has settled** on the ground and hardened into rock, this material is called tuff. Tuff may have features of sedimentary rocks, such as layers or strata. Ash that has settled in the sea may contain fossils of shellfish.

- **Ignimbrite** is a type of tuff in which the fragments are welded together, partly by quartz droplets. They are erupted from very violent Peleean volcanoes.

- **When Mt Pelee** on Martinique erupted in 1902, an ignimbrite flow covered the town of St Pierre, 8 km away, in a few minutes. The 30,000 inhabitants were buried under the welded tuff, which reached a temperature of nearly 1000°C.

▼ *Thin strands of lava called Pelee's hair form when the lava is blown by the wind.*

- **As droplets** and larger lumps of lava are flung into the air, volcanic bombs form. The red hot lava may spin as it falls back towards the ground, and so may cool in an elongated spindle shape.

- **Breadcrust bombs** are larger chunks of lava around which a skin, or crust, forms. The molten lava inside releases gas and the skin expands and cracks, giving the appearance of a loaf of bread.

- **Bombs** usually have a vesicular texture, being riddled with gas-bubble cavities.

- **In Hawaii**, a lava spray is forced through very small openings and blown into strands by the wind. The very thin hairlike glassy material is called Pelee's hair. Pelee is a mythical lady who is said to live inside the volcano.

▶ *Volcanic bombs are lumps of molten lava flung high into the air by a violent eruption.*

...**FASCINATING FACT**...
In 1815 the volcano Tabora, in Indonesia, erupted with such force that 30 cubic km of dust was blown into the atmosphere and carried worldwide. The dust masked the Sun and caused 1816 to be called 'the year without summer'.

Vesicles and amygdales

- **Many igneous rocks**, especially lavas that cool on the Earth's surface, contain large amounts of gas.

- **The bubble cavities in the rock**, caused by small pockets of gas, are called vesicles.

- **The word vesicle** comes from the Latin *vesica*, which means a bladder or blister.

- **Vesicles are originally rounded**, but if the lava continues to flow, they become oval and elongated.

- **These gas bubble hollows** are more common in basic lavas than in those of intermediate or acid composition. Much basalt is vesicular.

- **Vesicles give a rock** a rough and pock-marked appearance.

- **Amygdales are the mineral infillings** frequently found in vesicles. They can form at any time after the cooling of vesicular lava.

- **They are rounded or almond-shaped** mineral masses, commonly of quartz and a group of minerals called zeolites.

- **The term amygdale** comes from the Greek word *amygdale*, meaning almond.

- **The filling vesicles** of quartz amygdales are often in the form of banded agate.

◀ *This specimen of basalt from Hawaii is full of vesicles. These are small holes made by gas bubbles in the molten lava.*

Rock columns

- **In many parts of the world** there are famous igneous rock formations where the rock is in almost perfect vertical columns. These include The Giant's Causeway (Antrim, Northern Ireland), Waikato Dam, (North Island, New Zealand) and Svartifoss waterfall (Iceland).

- **The columns** may be many tens of metres high and can be perfectly symmetrical and usually six-sided.

- **The igneous rock** involved is very often basalt, although dolerite, rhyolite and welded tuff may also form columns.

- **Columnar structures** are seen best in lava flows, but they also form less perfectly in sills.

- **Sills and lava flows** have vertical columns as they cool from the base and top. In a dyke, columns may develop horizontally as the rock cools from its vertical edges.

- **When a lake or pond** dries out, the wet mud on its bed shrinks into a pattern of polygonal cracks. Igneous rocks behave like this but in a more regular way.

▼ *The Giant's Causeway in Northern Ireland is a mass of interlocking basalt columns.*

▲ *The vertical columns on the Isle of Staffa, Scotland, have a mass of uneven lava above them. The dark opening is Fingal's Cave.*

- **The processes** that allow such regular shapes to form in cooling rock probably involve contraction and an even loss of heat throughout the rock.

- **As a lava flow** ceases to move, it begins to cool and form solid igneous rock. The base cools regularly and contraction begins to occur. Cracks develop and columns grow up through the lava.

- **Columnar formations** usually have a more perfect lower part and a less regular shape towards the top.

- **A hexagonal shape** allows the columns to fit together perfectly, but there can be columns with three to eight sides.

Rock pillows

- **Rounded masses of lava** called pillow lavas are well-known in the geological record.

- **The Earth's ocean floors** are made of basalt lava with a thin covering of sediment. Fresh basalt lava is continually erupting along the mid-ocean ridges.

- **On the deep seabed**, the composition of basalt lava is changed to form a rock called spilite. This may be because of chemical reactions between the lava and sea water.

- **The 'pillow' shape** of the lava masses is caused as a glassy skin cools around each mass of lava. Inside this skin, molten lava continues to move, giving the rounded shape.

- **The lava** may contain gas that enlarges the pillows and also gives the rock a special texture. Gas-bubble holes are left in the lava after the gas has escaped. This is called a vesicular texture.

- **The vesicles** in pillow lavas usually occur in rings that follow the pillow shape. In other lavas, they are randomly situated.

- **On the deep seabed**, pillow lavas are found with other rocks. Often they occur with mudstones.

- **Pillow lava** can also form when basalt erupts into wet mud, or below an ice sheet.

- **The spaces** between the pillows may be filled with broken lava fragments or a rock called chert. This is a very hard, silica-rich material.

- **Pillow lava occurs** in many parts of the world including Britain, south-east Germany, Washington, USA and North Island, New Zealand.

▲ *These metre-sized pillows were formed on the deep seabed over 500 million years ago.*

Geothermal springs

- **In many areas** where volcanic activity takes place (or has recently occurred), there are hot springs, or geysers.

- **The word 'geyser'** comes from the Icelandic *geysir*, meaning a 'spouter' or 'gusher'. In Iceland, there are a number of regions where heated underground water gushes to the surface.

◀ *The Old Faithful geyser in Yellowstone National Park, USA, flings steam into the air every hour.*

- **Hot water** from underground is used in Iceland for central heating and heating greenhouses in which fruit, vegetables and even bananas are grown.

- **In many regions** – such as California, USA, Weiraki, New Zealand, and Larderello, Italy – projects have been established to try to generate electricity from underground steam.

- **An individual geyser** consists of a central pipe with many branches leading from it at depth. Water heated volcanically underground becomes pressurized. As the mass of water boils, it bursts vertically through the central pipe and into the air. Some geysers erupt 70 m into the air.

- **A number of geysers** are very regular in their spouting, and they remain constant over many years.

- **On the surface**, a geyser is surrounded by a pool of silica-rich water at a temperature of about 85°C. Deposited in this and around its margins is a silica rock called geyserite, which makes a mound around the opening.

- **A fragment of wood** taken from the geyserite surrounding the Old Faithful geyser in Yellowstone National Park, USA, has been dated at 730 years old. This suggests how long that geyser has been spouting.

- **The geyserite** deposited around geysers at Rotorua, New Zealand has built the famous pink and white terraces.

> **...FASCINATING FACT...**
> The Romans appreciated the value of
> hot springs for bathing and laundry.

Uses of igneous rocks

- **Because of their attractive** crystalline surfaces, igneous rocks such as granite and porphyry, are cut and polished for use in buildings. These rocks are frequently found as facings in office blocks, banks and other commercial buildings.

- **Many granites** and related rocks have large crystals of pink and white feldspar, which give the rocks an attractive appearance.

- **It is currently fashionable** to use 'so-called' granite for kitchen work surfaces. The dark-coloured igneous rocks used in this way are actually syenites, not granite.

- **The appearance of igneous rocks** is often copied and printed onto other material for use as flooring and surface coverings.

- **Larvikite**, a type of syenite, is especially attractive. It is made of a mass of blue-grey feldspar crystals, which have a distinct silvery sheen.

- **Many igneous rocks** are also very durable. Rocks such as dolerite and basalt, are extensively quarried and then crushed to the required size or grade.

- **Road ballast** is a major use of crushed igneous rock. A kilometre of new road requires 10,000 tonnes.

- **Aggregate**, often made from finely crushed igneous rock, is used in concrete and building cement. The amount of aggregate required for a new office block may exceed 2000 tonnes.

- **As well as being physically strong**, igneous rocks are less susceptible to the effects of acid rain than other rocks, such as limestone.

● **Cemetries** provide examples of different igneous rocks in the form of polished gravestones.

▼ *Granite is often used for buildings as it has an attractive surface made of different mineral crystals and it is relatively resistant to weathering. Tower Bridge, spanning the Thames in London, is partly clad with Cornish granite.*

What are sedimentary rocks?

- **Sedimentary rocks** are best recognized by their layers. These bedding planes, or strata, result from the way the sediment has been deposited.

- **These rocks** are formed in a wide variety of environments on the Earth's surface, and in many cases are easier to study than igneous rocks, which often form at great depth in the Earth's crust.

Sandstone

- **Many sedimentary rocks** are made of particles that have been eroded or weathered from pre-existing rocks. For this reason, they are often referred to as secondary rocks.

- **The particles** are transported by rivers, wind, glaciers and gravity. During this journey they are changed and may become smaller, more rounded and broken.

- **Eventually**, when the transporting medium is no longer able to carry the sediment particles, they are deposited. A river, for example, can only carry large pebbles when it is flowing swiftly. As it slows down, so this material is left behind.

- **Most sedimentary rocks** are formed on the seabed. A river entering the sea slows down, depositing its load. The continental shelves have a great thickness of sediment, but much also reaches deeper parts of the oceans.

- **Sedimentary rocks** are of great importance. By looking at their detailed features and comparing these with how modern sediments are being formed, geologists can work out what our past environments were like.

- **Many sedimentary rocks** have great economic significance. Coal was the power behind the Industrial Revolution, and is still an important fuel, used for generating electricity.

- **Our knowledge** of evolution is based on fossil records. Fossils are preserved in sedimentary rocks.

- **Some well-known sedimentary rocks** include sandstone, limestone, mudstone or shale.

▼ *These high sea cliffs are made of sedimentary sandstone. The strata run almost horizontally.*

Weathering

◀ Tree roots grow into joints in many rocks. As the roots get larger, the rock is forced apart.

- **Rocks exposed** on the Earth's surface are broken down in many ways. Weathering causes rock decomposition without involving any movement, or transportation.

- **Weathering** is the first of many processes of denudation (wearing away). These processes result in an overall lowering of the land surface.

- **Many external agents** are involved in weathering, including temperature changes, rain, wind, bacteria, animals and plants.

- **Weathering** produces the particles of rocks and minerals, which are then transported and deposited as sedimentary rocks.

- **Mechanical weathering** is mainly the result of temperature changes. Water in cracks and joints in rocks expands when it freezes. This creates stresses, which cause rock disintegration. At the base of many mountain slopes and cliffs are scree slopes made of mechanically weathered fragments.

... FASCINATING FACT ...
Since the last ice age ended about 10,000 years ago, limestone pavements in North Yorkshire, UK, have been weathered vertically by half a metre.

◀ *When rocks are heated and cooled in deserts, flakes break off to leave a rounded core.*

● **Temperature changes** can cause the different minerals in a rock to expand and contract at different rates. Stress produced in this way may lead to thin sheets of rock peeling off like the skin of an onion.

● **Chemical weathering** affects many rocks. Limestones are particularly vulnerable. Rainwater is a mild, natural carbonic acid, and with increased acid rain, it becomes more acidic.

● **Limestone** itself is not soluble in rainwater. Calcium carbonate, of which limestones are largely composed, reacts with acid rainwater and soluble calcium bicarbonate is produced.

● **Granite**, often regarded as indestructible, is far from it. The most common mineral in granite is feldspar, which is easily weathered by acid water, especially in tropical conditions. The feldspar rots to clay and the granite is reduced to an incoherent mass of quartz and mica sand.

▶ *In cold climates, water in cracks in the rock turns to ice, forcing the layers apart and fragments are broken off.*

71

Erosion

▲ *A black moraine of eroded rocks snakes along this glacier surface in Iceland.*

- **Erosion** is the breakdown of rocks and wearing away of the land surface by processes that involve movement.

- **There are many different** environments in which erosion takes place, including rivers, glaciers, seas and deserts.

- **River erosion** occurs mainly where powerful, rapidly flowing streams cut deep valleys through the landscape. The valley sides are eroded, as is the rock debris carried by the water current. Much eroded sediment is carried to the sea where it is then deposited.

- **The power of river erosion** is well demonstrated by the depth to which the Colorado River has cut its deep V-shaped canyons in Arizona, USA.

- **A glacier** is less fluid than water, and so erodes a deep, reasonably straight valley that has a U-shaped profile. Eroded rock is carried on and within the ice, and deposited when the ice melts.

- **As a glacier moves**, rocks frozen into the ice scrape at the bedrock, eroding marks called striations into it. The ice freezes into cracks in the valley sides and plucks rock fragments away as it moves.

...FASCINATING FACT...
Wind laden with fine sand can strip
the paint from vehicles in an hour.

- **At the coast**, waves containing sand and pebbles break against cliffs and scour rock pavements. Cliffs are further reduced by landsliding, often assisted by water running over the cliff face or seeping from rocks.

- **In desert regions**, because of the lack of vegetation, the wind is the major erosive factor. Sand picked up by the wind blasts at any upstanding rock masses, concentrating near ground level. Rock pillars are sculpted by this abrasive wind, the weaker strata being eaten away more readily.

- **Larger rock fragments**, which are too heavy to be picked up by the wind, are etched and eroded into three-sided 'dreikanter'. Such pebbles are well-known from ancient sandstone deposits, and indicate a wind-dominant environment in the distant past.

▼ *Arches National Park, USA. The wind, carrying sand, erodes rocks into amazing shapes.*

How sedimentary rocks are formed

- **Weathering and erosion** provide the particles from which sedimentary rocks are made.

- **Sediments** may form into rocks with no alteration, by a process called lithification. When physical or chemical changes occur during rock formation, the process is called diagenesis.

- **Most sediment** is deposited in the sea. Initially it will be wet and the pore spaces between the grains filled with water. This must be removed to turn the sediment into rock.

- **As layer after layer** of sediment is deposited, the weight and pressure produced begins to affect lower layers. Water may be squeezed out, and the individual grains get packed together more tightly, reducing pore space.

- **When sediment** is first deposited in water, most of it (70–90 percent) is made up of small gaps between the grains. These gaps are called pore spores. As the sediment is buried deeper in the Earth's crust, the pore spores are reduced to only around 30 percent of the rock's volume.

- **In some cases**, where overlying weight is considerable, sand grains may become welded together, with the removal of pore spaces.

- **Many rocks**, like sandstone, do remain porous and may be a valuable source of underground water, gas or oil.

- **Mineral enriched fluids** seep into pore spaces and form natural cements that bind together the individual particles, including pebbles, in sedimentary rocks. A common cement is calcite (calcium carbonate).

- **Quartz** (silicon dioxide) is another common cementing mineral. This hard, chemically resistant cement is common in many sandstones.

- **Limestones** are largely made of calcite, often derived from organic matter. They may be packed with shell fragments, broken crinoid stems or corals. Recrystallization may occur and the organic material is dissolved, to be replaced by a mosaic of crystalline calcite.

- **Many sediments** undergo colour changes as they harden. Iron compounds seeping into pore spaces may colour sandstone red or yellow.

◀ *These layers of sand and pebbles may one day become sandstone and breccia.*

75

Environmental evidence

- **Sedimentary rocks** contain evidence that geologists can use to identify the type of environment in which the rock was originally deposited. The rock may have been deposited in the deep ocean, on a beach, glacier or in a desert.

- **Each environment** leaves behind tell-tale clues in the rock. Geologists need to look at a range of evidence in order to accurately determine the depositional environment of the rocks.

- **The size of the grains** in the rock is a good starting point. On a beach, there are large pebbles, and out in the sea, mud, silt and sand. Powerful water currents are needed to carry large grains of sediment, and only fine mud can be taken into the deepest oceans.

- **On wet sand**, towards the low tide mark, the sea makes regular patterns called ripple marks. Similar structures are common on sandstone strata, suggesting that these rocks may have been deposited between the tides, by moving river water or by wind in desert environments.

- **A pattern** of joining cracks is made when mud dries out, for example, on the edge of a lake. Such mud-cracks are commonly found on many strata. This suggests these rocks were formed from lake mud.

- **Mud cracks** can also indicate arid, desert environments. They can also form on tidal mudflats that dry up. Shrinkage cracks can also form in shallow water (usually sea water).

- **When a large river** flows into the sea, it may deposit a vast delta like that at the mouth of the Mississippi River in the USA.

▲ *This sandstone surface is 150 million years old. It has ripple marks on it that were made on an ancient beach.*

- **There are many** different sedimentary rocks in a delta. Across the delta run many smaller streams, which cut their valleys in the delta sand and mud. Channels carved into sandstones may suggest they originated in a delta.

- **If sandstone strata** are curved and not flat, then the rock may have been formed in a desert as the layers of sand in a dune are gently curved (cross-bedded).

- **Fossils** are often a good clue as to where the sediment was deposited. Some limestones contain fossil corals similar to those found in warm tropical seas today.

Sandstone

◄ *The small, rounded quartz grains making this sandstone are clearly seen in this specimen.*

● **Sandstone** is a common sedimentary rock. Essentially, it is made of sand grains compressed together, or cemented by other minerals.

● **Sandstones can be created** in a variety of environments. Some are formed in deserts, some on the seabed, and others in rivers and deltas.

● **Sand grains** blown by the wind tend to be rounded and slightly frosted in appearance. Those carried and deposited by water are usually more angular.

● **The main mineral** in sandstone is quartz. This material is chemically and physically resistant, so is readily able to withstand being transported some distance before being deposited.

● **Some sandstones** contain a relatively high proportion of feldspar. One example is a rock called arkose. Feldspar is easily weathered, so its presence in sandstone suggests that the sediment was deposited quickly.

> ...FASCINATING FACT...
> On the bedding planes of certain sandstones small glittery flakes can be seen. These are fragments of the mineral called mica.

- **Sandstones** generally do not contain as many fossils as other sedimentary rocks such as limestones. However, sandstones formed in the sea can contain mollusc and brachiopod shells, trilobites and ammonites. Delta sandstones contain plant fossils and some of the best dinosaur fossils are from sandstones formed in river beds and on land.

- **There are many** colour varieties of sandstone. These are mainly due to minerals in the rock, some of which cement the sand grains together.

- **Red and yellow** sandstones contain the minerals hematite and limonite around their grains.

- **Sandstones** are economically important. They are used for building as many of them can be cut easily into stones. Porous sandstones can hold water, oil or gas underground, which can be extracted by means of boreholes.

◀ *The sandstone in these strata are red-coloured because of hematite (iron oxide) on the quartz grains.*

Strata and folding

▲ *When rocks are highly compressed, tight folds can be formed.*

- **Many sedimentary rocks** are deposited in neat layers that geologists call strata. Each stratum represents the seabed or land surface at the time it was deposited. The term 'bedding planes' is also used for strata.

- **Fossils** may be found on strata. When deposition stops for any length of time, animals and plants may live on the sediment surface, and their remains will be covered over and preserved when deposition resumes.

- **One of the main** principles of geology is that as strata are formed, the oldest one, the first to be deposited, will be at the bottom and the youngest, the most recently formed, will be at the top.

- **If there is continuous** deposition of sediment, then there will be no strata. Sedimentary rocks without strata are said to be massive.

- **Strata** can be linked from place to place by using the fossils they contain. The same ammonite fossils found in mudstone in Greenland, shale in Argentina and limestone in Italy prove that these strata are the same age.

- **The layers of** sedimentary rock were originally deposited horizontally. As the Earth's crust moves, so these layers may be tilted and folded.

- **Though many younger** strata are more or less horizontal, older ones are usually folded. However, the Torridonian sandstones in north-west Scotland are over 900 million years old and have never been folded.

- **Geologists** measure features of folded strata when they make geological maps. The greatest angle that can be measured down a sloping stratum is called the dip of the stratum. This is indicated on a geological map with a small arrow pointing in the direction of the dip and a figure for the angle.

- **When the pressure** is greater from one direction, the folding will be uneven and one side of the fold may even tilt over above the other. This is a recumbent fold. Structures such as these are common in the great mountain ranges such as the Alps and the Andes.

> ...FASCINATING FACT...
> Compression of the crust buckles strata into upfolds (anticlines) and downfolds (synclines).

Conglomerate and breccia

▶ *Breccia is made of large fragments of sedimentary deposits stuck together.*

- **Conglomerate** is the name geologists give to a sedimentary rock made of large, rounded fragments.

- **Usually**, the pebbles and other fragments are held together with a cement. This may be quartz, calcite or iron compounds.

- **The pebbles** themselves can be made of many materials. There may be rock fragments that have been eroded and heaped together. Many conglomerates contain pebbles of quartz or quartzite.

- **Conglomerates** are usually deposited near to the area from which their fragments were eroded. Many conglomerates were deposited by rivers. This is because it takes a powerful river current to move such large particles.

- **Many conglomerates** are beach deposits. The fragments will be well-rounded because of being rolled backwards and forwards by the waves and tide.

- **Some conglomerates** are the deposits of flash floods in predominantly arid areas. Great masses of sand and pebbles lying on the land surface are easily washed along by powerful floods.

- **Breccia** is a rock that is similar to a conglomerate. However in breccia, the fragments are jagged and angular.

- **Breccia** is deposited very quickly, sometimes without water transport, so the pebbles and other fragments it contains don't get worn and rounded.

- **Many breccias** are formed as scree by the weathering of high mountain slopes.

- **Rock fragments** are produced when rocks move relatively to each other during faulting. The jumble of broken rock along the fault line is called fault breccia.

▶ *These layers of conglomerate were formed on a river flood plain, when masses of pebbles were carried and deposited by turbulent water, over 200 million years ago.*

Bone bed

- **At a number of points** in the geological record there are strange, highly fossiliferous layers of rock called bone beds.

- **Bone beds are usually quite thin**, and contain a lot of pyrite and phosphate.

- **The rock containing the bone** and other fossil fragments is usually limestone, sandstone or conglomerate.

- **The term bone bed** refers to the fossil content of the stratum. Bone fragments, fish scales and teeth, and coprolites (fossil dung) are often concentrated in bone beds.

- **Probably the best-known bone bed** in Britain is that which occurs in the youngest part of the late Triassic Period on the Severn estuary. This is referred to as the Rhaetic bone bed. It contains dinosaur, fish and marine reptile fossils.

- **Bone beds are called condensed deposits**, partly because they contain very little sediment in relation to the masses of fossil fragments.

  - **The masses of fossils** may be due to local extinctions, or the accumulation of fossils brought together by water currents.

    - **Remains of land and water creatures** that have been brought together by storms are found in some bone beds.

      - **Much of the material in a bone bed** is often coated with pyrite (iron sulphide).

        - **Some bone beds** contain large amounts of phosphate, which may be used as a fertilizer. Pebble-rich, phosphatic bone beds occur in Florida, USA.

◀ *In this specimen from Gloucestershire, UK, brownish fragments of fossil bone, black fish scales and other vertebrate fossils are set into a matrix of grey sediment.*

Time gaps – unconformities

- **Sedimentary strata** are not deposited continuously. Throughout geological time, there have been considerable gaps in deposition, and often older rocks have been removed by erosion before newer ones have formed.

- **A break** in the geological record is called an unconformity. These are rather puzzling features for a number of reasons.

- **The unconformity** is a rock surface. Below it the rocks may be very different – and much older – than the ones above.

- **Rocks below** an unconformity may be metamorphosed. The rocks above it may be ordinary-looking sedimentary rocks.

- **Geological time** has been recorded for us by events in the rocks. An unconformity represents a break in this record of time.

- **In the far north-west** of Scotland is one of the classic unconformities. The unconformity surface is an old, rough land surface. Below this surface are highly metamorphosed rocks dating back over 2600 million years. Above the unconformity are stratified sandstones. These are around 900 million years old. This means that 1700 million years of geological time are not recorded here.

- **Often geologists** can only suggest what might have happened during the time gap at an unconformity. Mountain ranges may have come and gone. Oceans may have flooded the area and disappeared. Sometimes evidence from other, nearby sequences, where more of the rocks have been preserved, can give some clues.

- **Very often**, an unconformity represents a time when much erosion took place. This removed many strata and with them our record of geological time. Then new rocks were deposited on the erosion surface.

- **Rocks** may be folded or tilted before they are eroded. If this occurs there will be a sharp angle between the older rocks and those above the unconformity. This is known as angular unconformity.

- **When the rocks** below and above an unconformity are similar, fossils help geologists to determine the relative age of each set of strata.

▶ *The bottom half of this cliff is made of steeply sloping layers of slate – the top half is limestone. Between the two is an unconformity where the slate was eroded to a flat surface before the deposition of the limestone.*

Manganese nodules

- **In the 1870s**, scientists on the research vessel *Challenger* discovered strange lumps, or nodules, of rock on the beds of the Atlantic and Pacific Oceans. As much as 35 percent of the nodules were made up of the metal manganese. The scientists called them manganese nodules.

- **Each nodule** is rather like a potato in size and shape. The outer surface is rough and uneven, and when dry, is dark brown and dusty.

- **Inside**, the nodules are complex. They have an onion-like layering, built up around a grain of sediment or a fossil fragment. It has been proved by radiometric dating that it takes 40 million years for a 10 cm nodule to develop.

- **Manganese** is only one of many important metals found in the nodules. They also contain copper, nickel and cobalt.

- **An extensive survey** of the Pacific Ocean bed was carried out in 1962. This survey found a vast deposit of manganese nodules at a depth of around 5000 m.

- **Manganese nodules** are also found in the southern Atlantic Ocean, the Caribbean Sea area and the southern Indian Ocean.

- **Mining at sea** for the nodules has been carried out by the United States. The ship *Deepsea Miner* dredged the Pacific floor and recovered many tonnes of nodules in the late 1970s.

> ...FASCINATING FACT...
> Manganese nodules are a source of metals.
> Manganese and cobalt are used in alloys for the oil
> refining industry. They are also used in jet engines.

- **There are problems** with mining from the deep ocean floor. Even using computerized controls to position the ship, the venture has so far proved very expensive.

- **It is estimated** that 5500 tonnes of nodules would have to be recovered every day to make mining worthwhile. The environmental impact of this on deep marine life and the environment would be considerable.

▲ *The curved layers can be seen in this broken manganese nodule. This specimen was dredged from the seabed 5000 m down in the Pacific Ocean near the Marquesas Islands.*

Deep-sea sediment

▲ *When deep-sea ocean sediments are deposited by turbidity currents, they often result in fine and coarser layers as in these sloping strata. Turbidity currents are rapidly moving masses of sand and mud that flow along the deep seabed.*

- **In the deepest part** of the ocean basins, thousands of miles from land, strange sedimentary deposits accumulate. This region is often referred to as the abyssal part of the oceans.

- **Some sediment** that turns into sedimentary rocks is deposited on the broad continental shelves (the shallow margins around some of the continents).

- **Because the ocean** doesn't have the force to carry sand and pebbles, these are left behind near the shore. Only the finest mud and clay usually travels far out onto the ocean floor. This is carried in suspension in the sea water and only very gradually settles to the seabed. Geologists use the term 'ooze' for this dustlike sediment.

- **Icebergs** have been known to float far away from their polar origins. Trapped in these huge blocks of ice is sediment. This can be in the form of clay and sand or giant boulders. Eventually, as the iceberg or ice melts, these are dropped to the deep seabed.

- **Volcanic dust** is often flung high into the atmosphere to circulate in the wind systems. This dust can settle into the oceans and onto the deep seabed.

- **Ocean water** is filled with countless organisms and their skeletons are often made of calcite. These accumulate to make up calcite-rich ooze. This process occurs to a depth of around 4000 m. Below this level, on the deepest ocean floors, this deposit is absent. Scientists have discovered that below this depth, calcite is dissolved in the sea water.

- **One unusual type** of sediment found in the deep ocean is made of repeated layers of sand and mud. It has been discovered that these are deposited by rapidly flowing seabed currents, carrying vast amounts of sediment from the land. As the current loses its force, the sand is deposited first and then the mud, giving the alternating layers. Geologists call these currents turbidity currents.

- **In the geological record**, there are thousands of metres of dark, very fine sediment, called mudstone. This rock may contain fossils of planktonic organisms. It is usually regarded as a deep-sea rock.

- **Associated with dark-coloured shale**, geologists sometimes find repeated sand layers. These are proof that turbidity currents were at work in the past.

. . . .FASCINATING FACT. . . .
Marine organisms called diatoms and radiolarians
have skeletons made of silica. This material
accumulates on the ocean floor to make silica ooze.

Limestone

▶ *Limestone is often packed with fossils. Those shown here are the remains of water snails.*

- **Limestone** is a sedimentary rock that contains a high proportion of the mineral calcite (calcium carbonate). Often, this is of organic origin.

- **Limestones** are usually pale-coloured, being grey, cream, brownish or buff. Some are very dark and may be almost black because of a high percentage of mud and other eroded sediment.

- **Fossils** are abundant in most limestones. Some of these rocks are named after the fossils they contain. Coral limestone, crinoidal and shelly limestone are rich in these fossils. Limestone may be a mass of fossils cemented together by calcite.

- **Most limestone deposits** are geologically young. Organisms that developed hard calcite shells, from which the rock is often made, didn't evolve until Cambrian times. Pre-cambrian limestone is often made of calcite secreted by colonies of blue-green algae, forming mounds called stromatolites.

- **Chemical weathering** easily attacks limestone. The rock is etched into characteristic structures, and joints are enlarged as water runs through them. Underground cave and stream systems develop, and there is often a complete lack of surface drainage.

- **Dolostone** (dolomite) is a type of limestone in which much of the calcite has been changed into the mineral dolomite. Dolomite is a double carbonate of calcium and magnesium. It forms as the rock hardens.

- **Oolitic limestone** is made of small, rounded grains (ooliths) of sediment, about 2–3 mm in diameter. These are of chemical origin and made of concentric layers of calcite. The layers are formed around a small shell fragment or sand grain. Today, oolitic limestones are forming around the Bahama Banks in the Caribbean.

- **Reef limestones** are fossilized sediment reefs. They contain a variety of fossils of organisms that live in the shallow reef environment. These may include corals, trilobites, brachiopods, molluscs and crinoids.

- **The reef** itself is a mound of sediment, the surface of which is near to sea level. Some reefs may be composed of a lime mud, secreted by various micro-organisms.

- **Limestone** has many important economic uses and is often extensively quarried. For many years it has been powdered for agricultural purposes. Limestone is an important building stone and forms the basis of cement.

◀ *Limestone landscapes often have much bare rock. This is because there is very little surface water so soil doesn't form and plants cannot grow.*

93

Limestone pavement

- **A limestone pavement** is an expanse of bare limestone that has taken thousands of years to develop and is usually criss-crossed by deep grooves.

- **In the British Isles**, limestone pavements are best known in the Yorkshire Dales and the Burren region of western Ireland.

- **Limestone pavements form** a significant landscape feature, and the deep cracks or fissures running through them, called grykes, are places where rare limestone-loving plants grow. The blocks of limestone between the grykes are called clints.

- **In recent years**, many limestone pavements have been destroyed. The limestone has been removed and sold for rockery and building stone.

- **The landscape features** of regions where limestone occurs at the surface owe their formation to the physical and chemical properties of the rock.

- **Limestone is mainly composed** of the mineral calcite, with the chemical composition of calcium carbonate.

- **Calcite reacts chemically** with weak acids in rain water and ground water to form calcium bicarbonate. This chemical compound is soluble in water, and so limestone is chemically weathered and removed.

- **Chemical weathering** of limestone is concentrated along bedding planes and vertical joints. These are enlarged, and surface water easily runs underground. Such rocks are said to be permeable.

- **Surface water is lacking** in many limestone regions, which means soil development and plant growth are very limited, and bare rock occurs at the surface.

▶ *In this limestone pavement in the Pennines of North Yorkshire, UK, the blocks of limestone called clints (1) are separated from each other by deep joints called grykes (2).*

- **It has been argued** that some limestone pavements formed below a surface layer of soil and peat. This would increase the acidity of water running through the limestone. At a later time, possibly after the last Ice Age, the peat was weathered and eroded to leave the bare limestone surface.

Oolitic limestone

- **Small, rounded particles** called ooliths make up oolitic limestone.

- **Ooliths are 1–2 mm in diameter**, and are composed of many concentric layers of calcite.

- **There may be a small shell fragment** or sand grain in the centre of each oolith.

- **The accumulation of calcite layers** around a nucleus in moving seawater form ooliths.

- **Between the ooliths is the rock matrix**, which is composed of calcite. This joins the ooliths together.

- **Oolitic limestone is usually grey** or pale cream in colour. It makes an attractive building stone.

- **Many types of this limestone** are well-bedded (stratified) and this feature helps with quarrying and working the rock.

◀ *Oolitic limestone has been quarried as building stone for many years. In this quarry face, horizontal bedding planes can be clearly seen.*

- **This limestone is often rich** in fossils. It may contain the remains of corals, brachiopods, molluscs and echinoderms.

- **Today, oolitic limestone is deposited** on the Bahama Banks off the Florida coast, and in the Gulf of Suez between Egypt and the Arabian Desert. In these places, ooliths form in warm, moving, shallow water, about 7 m deep.

- **Pisolitic limestones** (from the Latin *pisum*, meaning pea) are similar to oolitic rocks, but the rounded grains are pea-sized.

97

Chalk

- **Chalk** is a special type of limestone. It is almost pure white, very fine grained and most contains over 90 percent calcium carbonate (calcite).

- **Chalk** is a sedimentary rock that was deposited in the sea, probably away from the continental shelf, in regions where there was little seabed disturbance.

- **Most chalk** occurs in western Europe and in some parts of North America, for example in the state of Kansas. European chalk was deposited during the Cretaceous Period between 142 and 65 million years ago.

- **The famous white cliffs** along the south coast of England, which for years have been a landmark for travellers, are composed of chalk.

- **One of the puzzles** about chalk is its great purity. There is an almost complete lack of sand or mud and other sediment carried from the land.

- **Much of the nearest land** was probably very low lying, without hills and mountains. Because of this there would have been very little erosion bringing mud or sand into the sea.

- **Virtually all the calcite** in chalk is the remains of small organisms. These include microscopic creatures called coccoliths.

- **Large fossils** are found in chalk. These include ammonites and other molluscs, brachiopods and echinoids (sea urchins).

◀ *Chalk is a white powdery rock made of the remains of minute sea creatures.*

▲ *Along the south coast of England there are many high chalk cliffs,*
as here at Bat's Head in Dorset.

- **The layers of chalk** are divided into time zones using ammonite fossils.

- **A variety of creatures** lived in and on the soft seabed. Worms and sea
  urchins burrowed into the chalky mud. Sponges and molluscs also lived on
  the seabed.

Flint

▶ *When carefully chipped, flint can be used to make tools such as this pointed hand axe.*

- **Flint** is a hard, nodular rock, found in irregular layers in chalk.

- **Flints** can be seen in chalk cliffs as dark parallel bands running among the white strata.

- **Like the common mineral quartz**, flint is composed of silicon dioxide. Quartz usually forms hexagonal crystals but flint is different. The crystals making up flint are so small that a powerful microscope is needed to see them.

- **The silica** in flint is derived from small sea creatures. It mainly comes from the internal supports of sponges. It is believed that concentrations of silica formed within the chalk sediment and hardened into flint.

- **Large fossils** are sometimes replaced by flint, such as the heart-shaped sea urchin called *Micraster*.

- **'False flints'** are hollow inside. Here the silica formed around a sponge, that eventually disintegrated, leaving a hollow. These false flints have a white powdery interior made from the shells of single-celled foraminferans and ostracods (creatures related to water fleas).

- **When flint** is seen on the surface of a chalk stratum, the nodular lumps may occur in rings.

- **Flint** is so hard that it can't be scratched with a knife blade. It breaks easily into curved shapes with very sharp edges.

- **The durability and sharpness** of broken flint has been exploited in the past.

- **Early man** used flints to make hand axes from at least 2 million years ago. These were shaped by chipping flakes of flint from around a core, using a hammer stone. Flint has continued to be used in tools right up until the early 1800s when flintlocks were still being made.

▶ *Flint is often dark-coloured and breaks with sharp jagged edges. It is a very pure type of silicon dioxide.*

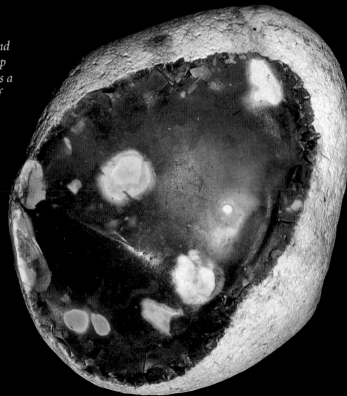

Ice age rocks

- **The most recent ice age** ended in Britain and most of Europe and North America around 10,000 years ago. Much evidence for this ice age can be found in the landforms created by the ice sheets and glaciers and in their special sedimentary rocks.

- **Glacial rocks** are known from much older times. There is evidence of an ice age that affected parts of Scotland in the Permian Era. Glacial sediments occur in Brazil that were formed during the Carboniferous and Permian Periods (355–250 million years ago). These are 1600 m thick in places, suggesting an amazing amount of erosion by the ancient glaciers.

- **As glaciers and ice sheets** move, they pick up fresh and eroded rock material. This is carried in, on and beneath the ice. Eventually, as the ice melts, deposition occurs.

- **A typical feature** of many glacial sedimentary rocks is that they are badly sorted. This means that within one deposit there will be fragments of many sizes, from fine clay to large boulders.

- **Glacial rocks** are commonly un-bedded. They do not have the neat strata that identify most sedimentary rocks.

- **The term moraine** is used to cover a wide variety of glacial deposits. It may consist of sand, gravel, clay and rock fragments. Much eroded rock debris falls along the sides of a glacier. This lateral moraine may be further eroded against the valley sides as the ice moves.

- **A push moraine** is bulldozed along at the glacier snout (front end). Any glacier may produce a number of these as it retreats and then re-advances. Terminal moraines usually form in this way, and give geologists evidence about the furthest position a glacier reached.

- **If two valley glaciers** join, their lateral moraines will merge to form a medial moraine in the new, larger glacier.

- **Much meltwater** is associated with glaciers. This flows out from under the ice carrying sediment. Usually meltwater is thick and milky-looking because of the clay it contains. The area in front of the glacier snout is called an outwash plain. Water-formed sediments occur here, often in neat strata.

- **The large boulders** (and other rocks) carried and dumped by the ice are often left stranded and out of place. These are called erratics, and their significance is considerable. By studying the erratics, geologists are able to tell from where a long-vanished ice sheet came.

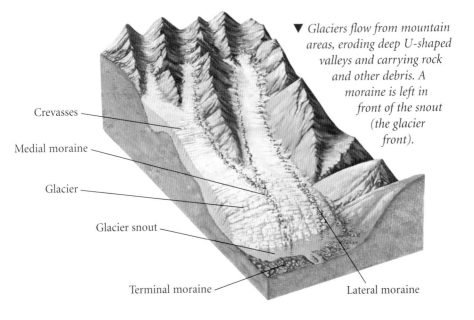

▼ *Glaciers flow from mountain areas, eroding deep U-shaped valleys and carrying rock and other debris. A moraine is left in front of the snout (the glacier front).*

Crevasses

Medial moraine

Glacier

Glacier snout

Terminal moraine

Lateral moraine

Coal

- **Coal** is the classic fossil fuel that provided power to the 19th century Industrial Revolution. It is the most abundant and easiest fossil fuel to recover.

- **Coal is the consolidated remains** of carbon stored in plants. These plants, living hundreds of millions of years ago, took in energy from sunlight and stored it in their tissues. When a light bulb is switched on, using electricity generated in a coal-fired power station, 'fossil sunlight' is being released.

- **Coal** is most common in strata of the Carboniferous Period (355–298 million years ago). It is found in rocks from the Permian Period (298–250 million years ago), in South Africa, Brazil, China and Australia and in rocks from the Triassic Period (250–208 million years ago) in China and eastern USA.

- **Coal from** the Jurassic Period (208–144 million years ago) has been mined in England, northeast Scotland, Siberia and China. Rocks containing coal from the Cretaceous Period (144–65 million years ago) occur in Siberia, northern Germany and Canada.

- **The coal-forming plants** of the Carboniferous Period developed from peat deposited in the sedimentary layers of sand and mud formed on a vast delta.

- **Peat** is the first stage in the development of coal. This is a brown, often very waterlogged, material which has formed from partially decayed plant matter. For peat to be a useful fuel it has to be cut into blocks and dried.

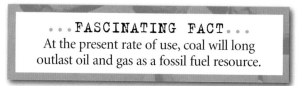

> ...**FASCINATING FACT**...
> At the present rate of use, coal will long
> outlast oil and gas as a fossil fuel resource.

- **In some parts of the world,** peat is used for domestic heating. It is burnt in power stations in some countries, such as Ireland.

- **As peat is buried** under more accumulated sediment, it becomes compressed and heated. The increase in temperature drives off impurities, including water. Gradually, the percentage of carbon in the peat increases, and it becomes (brown) lignite and then coal.

- **Bituminous coal** contains a far higher percentage of carbon than lignite and is the most widely used coal, but produces much ash.

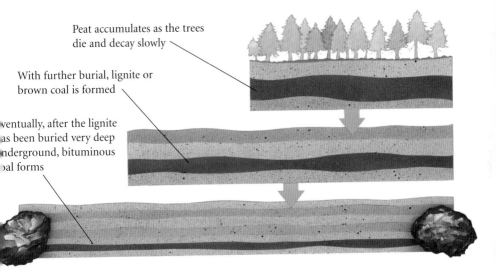

Peat accumulates as the trees die and decay slowly

With further burial, lignite or brown coal is formed

Eventually, after the lignite has been buried very deep underground, bituminous coal forms

▲ *Most coal was formed from trees and other vegetation living in swampy conditions. The dead trees formed peat as they rotted very slowly and eventually after being buried and heated under thousands of feet of rock, the peat turned to coal.*

Oil and gas

- **Oil and gas** are fossil fuels. Natural gas, commonly found with oil, has in many places taken over from coal gas as an important domestic and industrial fuel.

- **Oil** has given wealth to many nations that otherwise were poor.

- **Oil is a mixture** of many different hydrocarbons (compounds made largely of hydrogen and carbon) derived from marine organisms.

- **Oil and gas** are very mobile and move, under pressure, through strata, away from where they were formed.

- **Usually**, oil and gas are 'trapped' below ground. They move upwards through porous or permeable strata. Limestone and sandstone are good at allowing this movement. Eventually the moving fluids may come to a non-porous layer such as mudstone. Their movement is halted. The oil and gas then accumulate in the porous strata below the cap rock in an oil 'trap'. The strata containing oil often lie on top of strata containing brine (highly salted water) and gas occurs above the oil-rich layer.

▶ *Significant reserves of oil and gas have been discovered in the rock under the seabed. The fossil fuel is obtained using oil rigs – large platforms anchored to the seabed.*

- **Oil and gas** may eventually leak out onto the Earth's surface. When this happens, no geological exploration and surveying is needed to find the fossil fuels.

- **Oil does not always flow up** to the surface, and in many oilfields it has to be pumped to the surface by machines called 'nodding donkeys'.

▲ *A 'nodding donkey' pumping oil from Jurassic strata.*

- **When geologists** go out prospecting for oil, they look for structures where oil may be trapped. Areas where there is little soil and vegetation can be photographed from the air and structures show up readily. On the ground, porous strata can be detected below the surface by measuring the electrical resistance of rocks or their reaction to shock waves from small explosions.

- **Most oil** is discovered by drilling boreholes. Drilling for oil requires a lubricant called drilling mud. This keeps the drill bit cool. It is commonly made of heavy minerals and volcanic clay.

- **In some areas** such as the North Sea, oil was not found in the areas first prospected. Gas was present, however, and this became an important resource in the 1960s.

Evaporite rocks

- **The term 'evaporite'** is used for a range of rocks deposited from salt water. Rock salt (halite), rock gypsum and potash are the three most common and economically important evaporite rocks. Geologists classify all these deposits as chemical rocks.

- **The main evaporite deposits** exploited for their chemicals are formed from minerals in sea water.

- **If part of the sea**, such as a bay or gulf, is cut off from the open ocean by a sand bank, it will begin to dry up, especially in a hot, dry climate. This is the start of evaporite formation.

- **Some evaporite deposits** occur where inland salt lakes have dried out.

- **In the sea**, a series of evaporite rocks is deposited in a definite sequence. The rocks are usually interbedded with mudstone, which contains a high amount of calcite (calcium carbonate).

- **Some of the evaporite chemicals** are more soluble in water than others. The least soluble form layers of rock first. The most soluble remain in solution until the water has virtually dried out. The first to occur as strata are often gypsum and anhydrite. Rock salt is the next to form, and finally a mixture of potash rocks.

- **Many evaporite deposits** are forming at the present time, especially in arid regions. These are usually processed where they occur.

- **Of the marine evaporates**, rock salt (halite) is essential for human and animal health. It has been in great demand for thousands of years as a food enhancer and preserver. Gypsum and anhydrite are used for making sulphuric acid and fertilizers and for plaster and plasterboard. Potash is used as the basis of agricultural fertilizers.

- **The evaporites** deposited in land-bound lakes include borax and nitrates. Borax is used in glass, paper and leather products. Nitrates are the basis of fertilizers, explosives and nitric acid.

- **In Britain** there are considerable evaporite (halite) deposits in Cheshire and also in North Yorkshire, where mines over 5 km deep go out under the North Sea. Other important deposits occur in Germany, the USA and Chile.

▼ *Potash is used on a large scale for making agricultural fertilizers. This mine, in the North York Moors National Park, UK is over 5 km deep and tunnels stretch out below the nearby seabed.*

Stalactites and stalagmites

- **The roofs** of many limestone caves are covered with hanging, icicle-shaped growths made of calcium carbonate. These are called stalactites. The structures growing on the cave floor are stalagmites.

- **Limestone**, which is a common sedimentary rock, is easily weathered by chemical processes. Acid rainwater changes the calcite in limestone into soluble calcium bicarbonate, which is carried away.

▼ *Straw stalactites develop where water rich in calcium bicarbonate seeps through many small openings in a cave roof.*

...FASCINATING FACT...
In western Ireland, a stalactite has
been found that is 6.3 m long.

- **Chemical weathering** of limestone along bedding planes and joints allows water to run underground. Passages are eroded by this water, and as they grow in size, cave systems develop.

- **In the British Isles,** limestone caves have been formed in north-west Scotland, Derbyshire, North Yorkshire, Gloucestershire, Devon and western Ireland.

- **The opening** on the surface down which water runs is called a pot hole. Gaping Gill pothole in North Yorkshire is 120 m deep.

- **Water dripping** from a limestone cave roof is full of dissolved calcium bicarbonate. This is deposited as calcium carbonate (calcite) as the water drips into the cave and in part evaporates. The calcite is deposited in concentric rings to form stalactites.

- **Stalagmites** usually form beneath a stalactite from water dripping off its tip. They are more stumpy and shorter.

- **Stalactites**, hanging from the cave roof tend to be slender. Some, known as straw stalactites, are very small, but some are huge and can grow to many metres in length.

- **Both structures** are made of many layers of calcite. If cut open, the concentric rings of calcite can be seen. Sometimes, a stalactite and a stalagmite will join together to form a column.

Superposition

- **Geology,** like any science, has a number of laws, or principles, which help scientists to interpret rocks. The principle of superposition is one of these.

- **William Smith** (1769–1839), an English canal engineer and pioneering geologist, established the principle of superposition.

- **In simple terms,** the law of superposition states that in a sequence of sedimentary rocks, the older rocks lie below the younger layers.

- **A geologist** in the field may have problems interpreting strata according to this principle. In extreme conditions, folding for example will overturn the beds of rock so that younger layers lie beneath older ones.

- **Similarly a 'thrust fault'** may force old rocks above younger ones, which is another reason why the principle cannot be applied.

- **There are a number** of ways in which a geologist can prove if rocks are the correct 'way up'. These need to be applied before the order of strata can be determined.

- **Each stratum** marks a break in the deposition of sediment. On its surface various marks may be made. These prove which way up it formed. The sediment may be rippled, like a modern beach. If sediment dried out, mud cracks would be formed.

- **Fossils of animals** such as mollusc shells in their burrows, can also be used to show whether the rocks are the correct way up.

- **Volcanic rocks** that contained much gas will have their vesicles (gas-bubble holes) at the top of a lava flow.

▶ *On this wave-cut platform, the older strata are closer to the sea and youngest ones on the land. Each stratum dips (slopes) towards the land and disappears below a younger (higher) layer.*

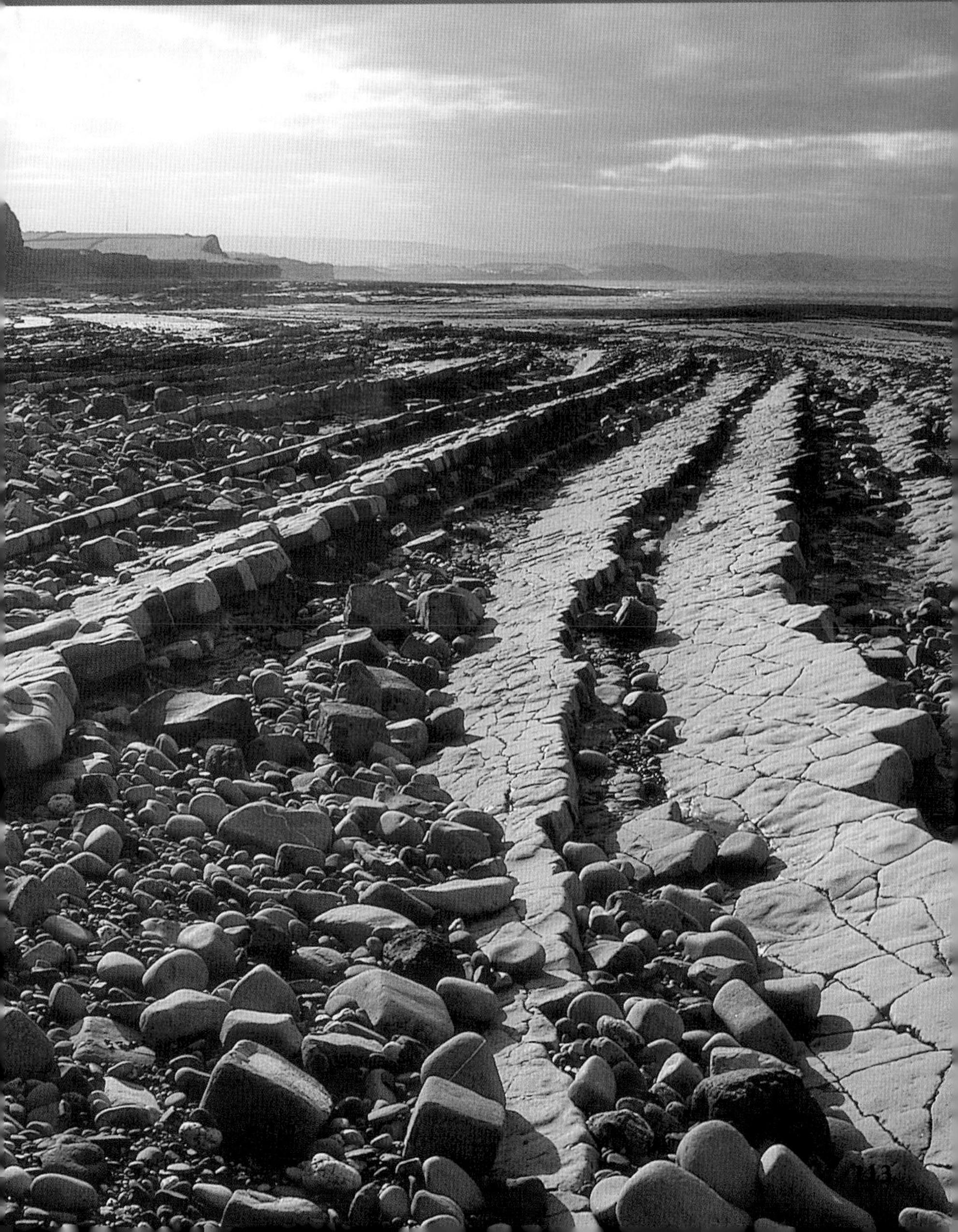

Ironstones

▲ *Banded ironstone is one of the richest ores of iron. This example comes from Western Australia.*

- **At least 90 percent** of all the iron mined and quarried each year is in the form of the sedimentary rock called ironstone.

- **Ironstones** formed in shallow water in the sea, near to land.

- **Iron** is one of the most sought after metals. It is used in the manufacture of steel, the main uses of which are in building and vehicle production.

- **The presence of iron** compounds in sedimentary rocks colours them red or yellowish-brown.

- **Some types of iron** are soluble in water and are carried to areas where sedimentary rocks are being deposited.

- **Iron** is easily oxidized (rusted) so is not very stable in today's climate. In the Precambrian Era (more than 600 million years ago), there was very little oxygen in the atmosphere, as there were no true land plants. Iron compounds were more stable at this time.

- **Very old rocks** of Precambrian age, which are rich in iron, occur in the USA around Lake Superior, Labrador in Canada, the Ukraine, Western Australia and Brazil.

- **Precambrian ironstones** are called banded ironstones because of their structure. They have thin, alternating layers of chert (a form of silicon dioxide) and iron oxide. These ores may contain up to 65 percent iron.

- **The ironstones** on which heavy industry was founded during the 19th century are of relatively low iron content – often less than 30 percent iron.

- **Many ironstones** have an oolitic structure, being made of small, rounded grains coated with iron minerals.

Rocks in the home

- **Slate**, a metamorphic rock that splits easily into thin slabs, is used for roofing in many parts of the world.

- **The walls** of buildings have been made of local stone of various kinds for thousands of years. The most suitable stones to use are 'freestones', which can be easily cut in any direction.

- **Attractive**, polished stones such as granite, syenite, marble and limestone are often used for mantlepieces and other decorative features such as facing stones.

- **Chimneys** may have liners made from clay to allow a smoother passage for smoke and reduce the risk of heat damage to stone or brick work.

- **Coal** is still used in many areas as a source of heating in the home. Electric power is largely generated by using this fossil fuel.

- **Plaster and plasterboard**, which are used to build interior walls, are made from the rock gypsum.

- **Cement**, which binds bricks, is made of limestone and mudstone.

- **Rock salt** is important as a flavouring for food. It is used in cooking, served as a condiment and is also used to preserve meat, fish and other foods.

- **The volcanic rock** pumice, is used for rubbing away dead skin.

- **Many kitchens** have a pestle and mortar for grinding food and spices. These are made from a variety of different rocks, including marble, granite and syenite.

- **Bricks** are made from a wide variety of mudstones, quarried thoughout the country.

◀ *Pool and snooker tables of high quality have their beds made of slate. This metamorphic rock can be split into perfectly flat layers and it doesn't warp when temperature or humidity changes.*

Aquifers

- **Many rocks**, such as sandstone and limestone, are porous. There are spaces or pores between the grains making up the rock, or there are joints, fissures and cavities that can all hold water.

- **Rocks** may also be permeable. These have joints and other cracks running through them that allow water to move underground.

- **An aquifer** is any rock that can retain or carry water and allow water to move through it. Aquifers are often very important sources of domestic and industrial water supply.

- **Water** held in an aquifer may sometimes flow out onto the surface.

- **The water table** is the level below which there is permanent saturation. It is not always the same level, and will depend on rainfall and river run-off.

- **Underground auifers** supply 25–30 percent of the water supply in England and Wales.

◄ *The limestone strata in these cliffs are permeable and allow water to run through and be held underground. When there is excess rainfall, the underground water level rises and springs form along a layer of impermeable rock near the foot of the cliffs.*

- **London** has a natural aquifer in the form of a syncline (downfold) of porous chalk. This structure forms the Chiltern Hills in the north, then dips below the capital and emerges as the North Downs to the south.

- **To obtain water** from an aquifer, boreholes are sunk. The water flows under pressure through these to the surface. Natural flow to the surface is called artesian flow.

- **In the past**, the pressure in London's aquifer was enough to supply the fountains in Trafalgar Square.

- **The sandstones** that date back to the Triassic Period, underlying Cheshire and Lancashire in the UK, form an aquifer in areas of heavy industry and high population.

◀ *Much of London's water supply comes from a natural aquifer of chalk dipping below the capital city.*

Deltas

- **A delta** is a mass of sediment built up at the mouth of a river where it enters a lake or the sea.

- **The Mississippi Delta** in the Gulf of Mexico, USA, has built up 'fingers' of low-lying land. Here, there is little tide or wave energy to move the sediment.

- **Sediment** is deposited when a river enters deep water because its speed and power to transport sediment suddenly decreases.

- **Deltaic rocks** include mudstones and sandstones. Coal seams may be found in sequences of deltaic rocks.

- **Because the top** of a delta is very close to sea level, a very slight increase in the sea level will cause flooding.

- **Millions of people** live and work on the Ganges and Brahmaputra delta region of north-east India and Bangladesh. Monsoon rains and storms in the Bay of Bengal often inundate the low-lying delta, with devastating results.

◀ *The Nile delta has many distributary channels between which are low lying areas of fertile river sediment called alluvium.*

> **...FASCINATING FACT...**
> Around 320 million years ago, much of Britain was submerged beneath a vast delta.

- **Many major oilfields** are in ancient delta rocks. These include the oilfields of Nigeria, the southern USA and the North Sea.

- **The building** of the Aswan Dam in Egypt has prevented sediment entering the Nile delta.

- **The marsh and water habitats** found on many deltas are home to a great variety of wildlife.

▲ *This sandstone was formed in a delta over 270 million years ago. The V-shaped mass of sandstone in the top half of the picture is the cross-section of a stream bed, which flowed across the delta, filled with sandstone.*

Desert rocks

▼ *Rocks formed in arid areas are often red or orange coloured. Here, in the Arches National Park, USA, the strata have been weathered and eroded into pillars and cliffs.*

Deserts are arid regions that receive very low rainfall, usually not enough to support vegetation.

Most desert regions are areas of high temperatures, but Antarctica is also a desert.

By studying the sediments and other features of today's deserts, geologists can work out which rocks were formed in ancient deserts.

Sandstone is one of the main desert rocks. The grains are rounded by wind action.

The strata formed by the wind are not horizontal. Instead, curved 'cross-bedded' layers are formed.

Larger fragments of quartz are often pitted and frosted by sand blasting.

Deserts are very windy environments, so mica, a mineral that occurs in small flakes, is absent from desert rocks.

If rain does fall on a desert region, it is usually very heavy for a short time. This creates flash floods, which can carry sand, pebbles and boulders.

'Desert rose' is a flower-like formation of the mineral gypsum that forms in deserts.

...FASCINATING FACT...
Many desert rocks are red-coloured because they contain iron oxide.

Concretions and nodules

- **Concretions and nodules** are rounded masses of rock found in many sedimentary rocks. They commonly occur in rows following the strata.

- **Most concretions** are a few centimetres in diameter, but some are measured in metres.

- **When they occur** in mudstone, concretions may be made of pyrite (iron sulphide), iron (siderite), calcite or phosphate.

- **Sandstone** often contains concretions that may be rich in iron compounds.

- **Flint forms** as nodules in the Cretaceous chalk. These dark masses are easily seen against the white rock.

- **Concretions** are often made of the same material in which they occur. They probably form after the sediment has been deposited, as it is turning to rock.

▼ *These rounded nodules in a Jurassic shale cliff are about 20 cm across. Often nodules such as these follow a particular stratum.*

▲ *These cracks have formed in a concretion as it has shrunk after formation. They are filled in with the mineral calcite.*

- **In some strata**, especially the lower Jurassic mudstones, concretions can contain well-preserved fossils. These are mainly molluscs such as ammonites.

- **A septarian nodule,** or concretion, is filled with radiating or concentric veins of mineral, often calcite. The veins occupy shrinkage cracks created as the nodules dry out.

- **Concretions and nodules** are usually more resistant to erosion than the mudstone in which they often occur.

Metamorphic rocks

▶ *Garnet is a mineral that forms in many metamorphic rocks, especially schist. It is used as a semi-precious gemstone and may be cut and facetted.*

● **Metamorphic rocks** are any rocks that have been changed by heat, pressure or a combination of these forces.

● **Most metamorphic changes** occur at temperatures of between 200°C and 700°C. The extreme pressure at which rocks metamorphose is up to 6000 times greater than atmospheric pressure and can occur at a depth of 20 km.

● **Contact metamorphism** involves only heat. Regional metamorphism is brought about by heat and pressure.

● **No melting of rock** occurs during metamorphism. When melting takes place, magma, from which igneous rocks are formed, is created.

● **The chemical composition** and structure of a rock can be changed by metamorphism.

● **When large-scale faulting** occurs, dislocation metamorphism takes place.

● **Original structures**, such as strata in sedimentary rocks, are removed during metamorphism.

Where rocks are highly folded, deep underground, they are altered by regional metamorphism. Rocks near to magma are changed by contact metamorphism.

Strata near to magma are changed by contact metamorphism

Layers of rock away from the heat remain unchanged

Rock can become folded and regionally metamorphosed

- **Fossils are sometimes found** in slightly metamorphosed rocks such as slate. As the degree of metamorphism increases, fossils are destroyed.

- **Garnet**, a mineral much used as a semi-precious gemstone, is common in the metamorphic rock called schist.

- **Some of the oldest rocks** in the Earth's crust are highly metamorphosed gneisses.

Contact metamorphism

- **Contact metamorphism** occurs when rocks are heated by magma or lava.

- **A metamorphic aureole** is the region around a mass of magma in which rocks have been altered.

- **A lava flow** can only metamorphose the rocks lying below it.

- **The amount** of contact metamorphism depends on the size of the igneous body producing heat and any fluids seeping from it.

- **The metamorphic aureole** around a large batholith may be a few kilometres wide.

- **A small sill**, dyke or lava flow may metamorphose rocks up to only a few centimetres away.

- **A gradual** metamorphic change takes place away from the igneous intrusion. The rocks furthest away are only slightly metamorphosed. Right next to the intrusion they may be highly altered.

- **Dark-coloured 'spots'** and clusters of minerals are a common feature of clay and shale that have been altered by contact metamorphism. With great heat, a tough rock called hornfels is formed.

- **When heated**, limestone becomes crystalline marble. This new rock is a mosaic of calcite crystals, often with veins of green or blue minerals.

- **Sandstone** is changed to a hard, crystalline rock called metaquartzite.

▶ *The sloping rock surface on the right is made of granite. When it formed deep underground nearly 300 million years ago, intense heat from the magma metamorphosed the dark hornfels on the left of the picture. The contact between the two different rocks is clearly seen.*

Marble

- **Marble** is formed by the contact metamorphism of limestone.

- **Heat** from an igneous intrusion or lava flow causes the calcite in the limestone to recrystallize.

- **Original features** in the limestone, such as strata and fossils, are destroyed, and an interlocking mosaic of calcite crystals forms.

- **Pure limestones** become very pale, often sugary, marbles, with very little colour veining.

- **Limestone**, that has impurities in the form of clay, other sedimentary material, and minerals are changed into colorfully veined marbles.

- **The metamorphic minerals** brucite, olivine, and serpentine can give marble a greenish coloring.

- **Olivine marble** has small patches of bright green or brown olivine. This is a silicate mineral formed by the heat of metamorphism.

- **For over 2500 years**, marble has been prized as a decorative stone. This is because it is easily shaped and polished, and has attractive coloring.

- **In the classical Greek** and Roman periods, marble was the main rock used for statues.

- **Michelangelo's** *David*, carved between 1501 and 1504, is one of the most well-known marble statues in existence.

▶ *The abandoned marble quarry on the Isle of Iona, western Scotland. Marble was quarried here and much was shipped to Europe. This quarry closed in 1914.*

Metaquartzite

- **When sandstone** is altered by contact metamorphism, it turns into metaquartzite.

- **Heat from** an igneous intrusion or lava flow causes the quartz grains in sandstone to grow and fuse together or recrystallised.

- **Metaquartzite** may have only faint traces of the original bedding, and any fossils in the original sandstone will have been destroyed.

- **Sandstone** is more resistant to metamorphic change than many other rocks because so much heat is needed to alter it.

- **Metaquartzite** is a pale-coloured rock, often with a sugary texture.

- **Sandstone** is a porous rock with small spaces between the grains. Metaquartzite is crystalline and non-porous.

- **Because it is largely made** of quartz, metaquartzite is a very hard rock. It is resistant to weathering.

▶ *Originally sandstone, this metaquartzite is now a mosaic of quartz crystals. The original layers in the rock have disappeared.*

Metaquartzite is quarried and used in the construction industry.

Metaquartzite is found very close to large batholiths. Smaller intrusions rarely have sufficient heat to change quartz-rich sandstone.

Though it is virtually 100 percent quartz, metaquartzite may contain feldspar and iron oxides in small amounts.

▶ *The pale-coloured metaquartzite in this cliff still has some of its original features – strata are visible.*

Hornfels

▲ *This hornfels in Cornwall, UK, has been twisted and folded on a small scale by pressure in the Earth's crust. The paler bands are rich in quartz.*

Formed by the action of direct heat on pre-existing rocks, hornfels is a metamorphic rock.

This rock often occurs very close to igneous rocks such as granite. The granitic magma is a source of great heat when it is being intruded.

As well as heat, high temperature liquids can seep from granitic magma and help to metamorphose the surrounding rocks.

Hornfels is a flinty, tough rock that breaks unevenly, often with jagged edges.

The exact composition of hornfels depends to a certain extent on the original pre-metamorphic rock. Usually quartz is a common mineral, along with mica.

This rock has medium to fine crystals, often with a granular texture.

Hornfels can be twisted and contorted into tight folds.

The conditions of metamorphism cause new minerals to form. These include cordierite, chiastolite and garnet.

Some minerals, including garnet and pyroxene, often occur in what geologists call porphyroblasts. These are isolated clusters of minerals within the hornfels.

...FASCINATING FACT...
Hornfelses are usually named after the important minerals they contain, for example, garnet hornfels.

Crushed rock

- **Large-scale faulting** causes rocks along the fault surface to be crushed and metamorphosed.

- **Fault breccia** is a rock made of angular broken fragments. It is common along many fault lines.

- **The crushed rock** formed when thrust faults move deep in the Earth's crust is called mylonite.

- **Mylonite** is made from the dusty rock 'flour' that is created as rocks are ground up along the fault plane. Larger fragments, often stretched out, are stuck into this.

- **If thrust faults** occur deep in the crust where temperatures are high, new minerals will grow in mylonite. Chlorite, mica, feldspar and epidote are common examples.

- **As the fault moves**, rock flour and minerals are stretched out to give mylonite its typical texture.

▲ *Mylonite seen very close-up shows minerals streaked out during its formation. The pale mineral here is quartz.*

- **Mylonite tends to break** in thin plates and slabs parallel to its texture.
- **Geologists** use the term 'cataclasis' for the processes that create mylonite.
- **Large-scale thrust faults** occur in areas of mountain building.
- **There are a number** of thrust faults, with associated mylonite, in the north-west Highlands of Scotland.

▼ *The Glencoul thrust fault, Sutherland, Scotland. The thrust plane is the sloping surface halfway up the hillside. The grey mass of rock above it has moved from the right along the thrust plane above younger rocks.*

Faulting

- **Faults** are breaks in the rocks of the Earth's crust where the rocks move relative to each other. The same stratum will be at a different level on each side of the fault.

- **A joint** is a break in the rocks where no movement takes place.

- **Both faults and joints** are often the places where hot, mineral-rich fluids rise through the crust. Important mineral reserves occur in this way.

- **The actual surface** where the rocks break and move is called the fault plane. In many faults, such as normal and reversed faults, the fault plane is very steep. Thrust faults have a fault plane sloping at only a few degrees.

- **When faults move**, earthquakes occur. Movement on the San Andreas Fault that runs through California, USA, threatens large cities such as Los Angeles.

- **A normal fault** is where the Earth's crust stretches and one mass of rock moves down a break – the fault plane.

- **If two normal faults** occur parallel to each other a block of the crust may sink between them. This is called a rift, or graben. The region of rift valleys in east Africa was formed in this way.

- **Where a reverse fault** occurs, the Earth's crust is made thicker by compression. One mass of rock is forced up the fault plane relative to the rocks on the other side.

- **In a tear fault**, there is virtually no vertical movement. Rock masses are moved sideways relative to each other.

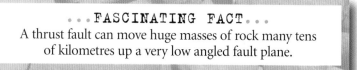

> ...FASCINATING FACT...
> A thrust fault can move huge masses of rock many tens
> of kilometres up a very low angled fault plane.

▼ Unlike most faults, the San Andreas Fault in California is visible on the Earth's surface.

Regional metamorphism

- **As the name implies**, this type of metamorphism occurs over great areas of the Earth's crust.

- **Regional metamorphism** happens when mountain building, often associated with movement of the Earth's lithospheric plates, occurs.

- **Pressure and heat** are involved in altering rocks by regional metamorphism.

- **The changes** that take place during regional metamorphism may take tens of millions of years to occur.

Gneiss

- **Some of the oldest rocks** in the Earth's crust have been affected by regional metamorphism. These have been radiometrically dated at over 3500 million years old.

- **The deeper** into the crust that rocks are taken by the processes of mountain building, the higher the degree, or grade, of metamorphism they suffer.

- **Rocks** formed by regional metamorphism are identified by their texture. Because of stresses in the rock, minerals are streaked out in layers.

- **High-grade rocks** – those that are altered most – are called gneiss. With increased temperature, caused by depth of burial, melting may occur and magma is created.

- **At lower depths**, where the temperature and pressure are lower, a rock called schist is formed.

Around the margins of the mountain region, temperatures are very low. Here, pressure is also low and rocks such as slate are created.

▼ *Regional metamorphism occurs in the roots of mountain chains. Deep below the Alps in Switzerland, slate, schist and gneiss are forming.*

Slate

- **Slate** forms around the margins of mountain regions where the lowest grade of regional metamorphism occurs.

- **Slates** are dark-coloured rocks made of grains and crystals too small to be seen with the naked eye.

- **The most recognizable feature** of slate is its cleavage. This is the way the rock splits into thin, neat layers. However, the most weakly metamorphosed slates may not have developed a cleavage.

- **Because it splits** so easily, slate has been used for hundreds of years for roofing and gravestones.

- **Fossils** may still be present in slate. These are often squashed or stretched by the stresses that metamorphosed the rock.

- **Slate** forms from the weak metamorphism of mudstone or siltstone.

- **Small, golden-coloured crystals** of pyrite (fool's gold) form in some slates.

- **Green slate** is coloured by the mineral chlorite, which grows under metamorphic stress.

- **Some of the world's** most important slate quarries are in North Wales. Slate from here has been shipped all over the world.

- **Slate** is also found in other parts of Britain, including Cumbria, Scotland and Devon. Elsewhere in the world, it occurs in California, USA, Onijarvi, Finland and Vosges, France.

This specimen of slate contains
crystals of pyrite (iron sulphide).
Pyrite often forms during
regional metamorphism.
The rock has broken along
a cleavage surface.

Schist

- **Schist** forms at higher temperatures and pressures than slate. These conditions occur deeper in the Earth's crust and nearer the centre of a mountain region.

- **Schist** is a silvery rock because it contains mica – this may be pale muscovite or dark biotite mica.

- **A typical feature** of schist is a wavy banding (called schistosity) running through the rock. This results from the way minerals have lined up during metamorphism.

- **As well as mica,** this rock contains quartz and feldspar.

- **Many new minerals** can form in schist during metamorphism. These include garnet, kyanite, hornblende and epidote.

- **Because temperatures** and pressure are moderately high when schists form, most rocks are altered.

  - **Garnet schists** are a source of the semi-precious gemstone, garnet.

  - **Much schist** occurs in the European Alps. Here, the rocks were folded and metamorphosed in mid-Cenozoic times, around 40 million years ago.

  - **In Britain**, schist occurs mainly in the Scottish Highlands, where it was formed during the Caledonian Period of mountain building, around 400 million years ago.

◄ *Schist has wavy bands running through it and this example has reddish garnet crystals.*

▼ *The hills and mountains of the Scottish Highlands are largely made of schist.*

Gneiss

▶ *The typical dark and light bands can be seen in this tightly folded gneiss specimen.*

- **Gneiss** is a rock formed by extreme heat and pressure deep within the Earth's crust. Under these conditions any previously formed rock will be completely changed. This is the highest grade of regional metamorphism.

- **During orogenies,** some rocks are buried to the depths at which gneiss forms.

- **Gneiss is characterised** by alternating dark and light coloured bands of different minerals. The mineral crystals are large enough to detect with the naked eye.

- **The pale bands** contain lower-density minerals such as quartz and feldspar, while the darker streaks contain denser minerals like biotite, mica and hornblende.

- **Some gneisses** may have isolated patches of other minerals such as red garnet. These can look like 'eyes' in the rock. This rock is called augen gneiss, from the German *augen*, meaning eyes.

- **The composition of gneiss** is not very different from that of the igneous rock granite.

146

Gneiss is generally the oldest rock in the area in which it occurs, and some gneisses have been radiometrically dated to over 3000 million years.

The major continental shield areas, such as the Canadian and Eurasian shields, are predominantly made of gneiss, with younger rocks on top.

Gneiss is a very durable rock. Its hardness is exploited in road making, and millions of tonnes of quarried gneiss boulders are used for coastal defences.

▼ *Gneiss forms a rugged landscape*
of low grey hills with much bare rock.

Eclogite

Eclogite is a rock that forms under high temperature and very high pressure in the deep roots of mountain chains.

It is a rare rock and is important because of what geologists can learn from it about the Earth's composition.

Eclogite contains large crystals easily seen with the naked eye.

The minerals in this rock may be arranged in alternating bands of different types or randomly scattered throughout its structure.

Eclogite is a dark-coloured rock made of yellowish or green pyroxene and red garnet.

Other minerals that occur in small amounts in eclogite include rutile, pyrite, corundum and kyanite.

Some eclogites are found in diamond pipes. They have been taken there from great depth by volcanic activity.

Geologists believe that eclogite gives important information about the rocks at the very base of the Earth's crust, and in the uppermost region of the Earth's mantle.

Experiments have shown that eclogite forms when basalt lava is melted and recrystallized under great pressure.

Eclogite occurs worldwide, especially in California, USA, the European Alps, Japan and South Africa.

◀ *Eclogite can be a most attractive rock, with masses of red garnet and green pyroxene. This example is from Norway.*

149

Building stones

- **In most parts of the world**, local stone is used for building. It is often possible to work out what the local geology is like by looking at what buildings, especially older ones, are made from.

- **Some rock types** are especially sought after because they are attractive, hard or easily cut into usable shapes.

- **Sandstone, limestone** and ironstone are three sedimentary rocks that are often used for building. Most of these can be cut easily and split along bedding planes. Rock without bedding (massive rock) can be more easily cut into the blocks required.

- **Though granite** is more difficult to cut than some sedimentary rocks, it has been quarried for building stone for hundreds of years. It is attractive and has good internal strength for structural supports.

- **Because stone used for buildings** is often cut and transported in large blocks, quarries developed in the 18th and 19th centuries were usually near good transport facilities.

- **The famous Aberdeen granite** quarries and the granite quarries in the Channel Isles and Cornwall were often sited near to the sea to make it easy to transport the quaried rock.

- **Warm-coloured limestones** of Jurassic age are used in southern England for many buildings. The well-known Portland limestone was brought to London from coastal quarries.

- **Limestone is readily attacked** by chemical weathering, and many buildings need restoration work when the stone suffers.

- **Slate is a tough**, easily split rock used for roofing.

- **Polished stone** often decorates the facades of offices and banks. Usually, granite or another coarse-grained igneous rock is used for this purpose.

▶ *The body of this cottage is made of small irregular-shaped nodules of flint, found in nearby chalk strata. The framework, window surrounds and lintels are brick.*

What are minerals?

- **A mineral** is a chemical compound or element that forms naturally in many different ways.

- **Most minerals** form inorganically, which means that living things play no part in their creation. However, some organic materials, such as amber, are usually classed with minerals.

- **Rocks** are made from minerals. Limestone is made mainly of the mineral calcite (calcium carbonate), and granite contains quartz, mica and feldspar.

- **Some minerals**, such as gold and diamond, are very valuable as currency or gemstones.

- **Geologists** tell one type of mineral from another by using special tests. Many of these are easy to carry out.

▶ *Minerals can be bright colours and have fine crystal shapes. The yellowish mineral is ettringite that forms as six-sided crystals. Here, dioptase is a rich green colour and the crystals have a vitreous (glassy) lustre.*

Many minerals form as perfect crystals. There is a great variety of crystal shapes, from simple cubes to complex dodecahedra with twelve faces.

Minerals can form irregular or rounded shapes without obvious crystals.

Some minerals are magnetic, others react with acids, and some are too hard to be scratched with a knife blade.

As well as occurring in rocks, minerals form in long narrow bands, called mineral veins, that run through the Earth's crust.

Minerals such as hematite (iron oxide), galena (lead sulphide) and salt (sodium chloride) are important industrial raw materials.

How hard are minerals?

- **Geologists** use a number of tests to tell one mineral from another. The hardness test is very useful in mineral identification.

- **The hardness** of a mineral depends on the strength of the forces that bind the atoms in the mineral together.

- **Gemstones**, such as diamond, ruby, sapphire and emerald, are very hard. It is difficult to scratch or damage them.

- **Mineral hardness** is measured according to how easily a mineral can be scratched. A mineral is tested by scratching it in turn with objects of increasing hardness, including the minerals on the hardness scale.

- **Geologists** use a special scale for measuring mineral hardness. It is called Mohs scale and was devised in 1812 by the German mineralogist Friedrich Mohs. There are ten points on Mohs scale, each one defined by a well-known mineral.

▼ *The ten-point hardness scale uses well-known minerals for its reference points.*

1	2	3	4	5
Talc	Gypsum	Calcite	Fluorite	Apatite

- **Talc** is the softest mineral at point 1 on the hardness scale. One form of this mineral is called soapstone and can be easily carved into ornaments. It can be scratched with a fingernail.

- **Diamond** is the hardest on the scale, at point 10. This highly prized gemstone is so hard that it is also used in industry as a cutting tool.

- **The other minerals** on the scale are; gypsum (2), calcite (3), fluorite (4), apatite (5), orthoclase (6), quartz (7), topaz (8) and corundum (9).

- **Certain everyday objects** are also used for testing hardness. A fingernail (2½), coin (3½) and knife blade (5½) are often used.

...FASCINATING FACT...
The first nine minerals on Mohs scale have roughly the same gap between them – that is, corundum is nine times harder than talc. Diamond, however, the tenth mineral on the scale, is 40 times harder than talc.

6	7	8	9	10
Orthoclase	Quartz	Topaz	Corundum	Diamond

Mineral colours

- **Minerals** range widely in colours, helping geologists tell them apart.

- **Mineral colour** depends on how light is reflected and absorbed by the elements in the mineral.

- **Quartz**, a very common mineral, can occur in many different colours. Amethyst is purple, citrine is yellow and the pink form is called rose quartz. Usually, quartz is grey or milky white.

- **Malachite**, which is a copper mineral, is a rich green colour, and azurite another mineral containing copper, is bright blue.

- **Common minerals** such as calcite, gypsum and barite are usually white.

- **Minerals** that contain iron, such as hematite and magnetite, are often reddish-brown or black.

◄ *Cinnabar is a bright red mineral that contains mercury.*

Gold is a wonderful rich yellow colour. Fool's gold (pyrite) is a similar colour, as is copper pyrite (chalcopyrite). It is easy to tell them apart using other tests such as hardness and specific gravity.

Cinnabar, a sulphide of mercury, is red, as is realgar (arsenic sulphide).

For thousands of years, mineral colours have been used as pigment in paints and dyes. Malachite was used as a green pigment over 2000 years ago in Egypt.

Ultramarine, a rich deep-blue colour, is made from powdered lazurite (lapis lazuli).

▶ *The brilliant green coating on this rock surface is the copper mineral conichalcite. Many minerals that contain copper are green.*

Gemstones

▶ *Small crystals of topaz growing into a hollow in an igneous rock. Topaz crystals can be cut and facetted as gemstones.*

● **Gemstones** have been prized for thousands of years for their rarity, colour, shape and durability.

● **There are only** a few dozen types of gemstones in everyday circulation. Other gemstones are too rare or soft to be of much use.

▶ *Ruby is a red variety of corundum and sapphire is the blue form. Emerald is a brilliant green variety of beryl.*

Ruby

Semi-precious gemstones include many colour varieties of quartz, such as purple amethyst.

Gemstones form naturally in many different geological situations. Some occur in igneous rocks, others in mineral veins or cavities.

Emerald

Because of their hardness, gems such as ruby and sapphire are not worn away by erosion in a river and so accumulate in river gravels and sands. These forms of corundum have been weathered and eroded from their original source.

Diamond is the best-known gemstone. Imitation diamonds have been made for many years. Rock crystal (quartz) and glass have both been used, but today materials such as cubic zirconia are produced as diamond substitutes.

Sapphire

To enhance their natural beauty, and remove imperfections, gemstones are cut and surfaces called facets are made.

A person who cuts and polishes gemstones is called a lapidary.

Gemstones, especially diamonds, are measured in 'carats'. A carat is a measure of weight, being 0.2 grams.

> ...**FASCINATING FACT**...
> The Cullinan diamond, discovered in South Africa in 1905, is the biggest diamond ever found. It weighed 3106 carats and was cut into 96 small stones and nine large ones.

Precious metals

- **Gold, silver and platinum** are all minerals that are precious metals. They occur on their own as 'native elements', which means they are not combined with other elements as compounds.

- **Gold** is easily recognized by its rich colour and great weight. It is 19 times heavier than an equal volume of water.

- **Gold is a soft metal**, easily scratched with a coin.

- **Found in a variety** of geological situations, gold occurs in veins, often with quartz. It occurs in river sand and shingle, where prospectors 'pan for gold'.

- **Native platinum metal** occurs as rare, silvery nuggets and minute grains with nickel and gold.

- **Platinum** commands a higher price on the world market than gold. It is used in catalytic converters, oil refining and jewellery.

- **Silver** is far less valuable than gold or platinum. When clean, it has a fine metallic lustre, but this rapidly fades and the metal becomes dull.

- **Silver** forms in delicate twisted wire shapes. Today, most silver is obtained from lead and copper mining and refining.

- **As well as being used** to make jewellery and ornaments, silver is a component of photographic film.

▶ *This small specimen of silver is a mass of interlocking wires. It has become tarnished and lost its bright metallic lustre.*

▲ *Gold is often found in quartz veins. This fine crystal of quartz has small flakes of gold on its surfaces.*

...FASCINATING FACT...
The ancient Egyptians were excellent goldsmiths. The boy king Tutankhamun's collar is made of worked gold.

Mining

- **The metals and fuels** on which we depend are mined or quarried from the ground.

- **Rock** that contains valuable material, usually metal, is called an ore. Hematite is an iron ore and bauxite is an ore of aluminium.

- **Over 3000 million tonnes** of metal and mineral ores are mined each year.

- **Ores are finite**, non-renewable materials. It is therefore important to recycle metals after use.

- **Metal ores** exist in many different geological settings. How they are mined largely depends on the size and shape of the deposit.

- **If an ore body is large** and in rocks that are structurally strong and occurs at depth, an underground mine will be used.

- **Surface (open pit) mining** is cheaper to carry out than underground mining. It can also produce far more ore in less time.

- **If the ore** is in loose surface sediments, it can be mined by using high-pressure water jets. Settling tanks may be used to separate the heavy ore from unwanted sand and clay.

- **Coal mining** was once a major industry in Britain, with hundreds of mines. Today, because of the low price of foreign coal and the use of other fuels, only a handful of mines are still working. Coal is also extracted by opencast methods.

▶ *Bauxite is an important ore of aluminium. This metal is strong and lightweight and doesn't rust like steel.*

Old mine workings and spoil heaps are excellent places to look for mineral specimens, if care is taken and permission sought from the landowner.

▼ *Mines are often in remote places. This small mine is extracting fluorite, which is used as a flux in steel making.*

Looking for minerals

◀ *In the 19th century, gold panning was an important way of obtaining the precious metal. This machine, called a cradle, was used to shake and wash sand that may have contained gold. The heavy grains and nuggets of gold were left behind as the lighter sand was washed away.*

- **Prospecting for mineral deposits** has become a refined science using many advanced techniques. It still relies, however, on certain proved methods, including field mapping.

  - **Field mapping** involves mapping rock structures on the ground. The use of aerial photography and satellite imagery, especially in regions with little vegetation cover, is useful for seeing such structures.

- **Many mineral deposits** are below ground. These can be investigated using what are called geophysical methods.

- **Rocks and minerals** have a property called specific gravity. This can be measured remotely from the surface. Metal ores usually have a high 'gravity' and are readily detected.

- **Iron deposits** often have a strong magnetism. In the 17th century, prospecting for iron ores was done using a compass! Modern magnetometers are so refined, they can measure slight changes in magnetism.

- **Geochemical analysis** of river sediment will detect metals that occur in valuable concentrations in the rocks the river has eroded.

- **Using a scintillometer (Geiger) counter** in the field may indicate concentrations of radioactive minerals such as uraninite

- **Mineral deposits** may be weathered and altered on the surface. Water that seeps underground can carry minerals and concentrate them at depth.

- **Gold, rubies and sapphires** found by panning in river sand may indicate the presence of more of these minerals upstream.

◀ *Minerals often occur in veins. Here, a metre-wide quartz vein runs across dark-coloured slate.*

Crystals

▶ *A fine group of small, reddish, six-sided vanadinite crystals.*

- **Many minerals** can form as crystals. These have surfaces that often join together perfectly.

- **Crystals** show symmetry. As a crystal is turned round, the same shape may be seen a number of times.

- **Mineralogists**, scientists who study minerals and crystals, classify crystals into a number of 'systems', according to their symmetry. The most symmetrical crystal system is called the cubic system.

- **Not all minerals** that form within a certain system will have the same crystal shape. In the cubic system there can be many shapes, including cubes and octahedra (eight-sided crystals). These shapes share the same symmetry.

- **The shape of a crystal** results from the way the atoms it is made of are fixed together.

```
...FASCINATING FACT...
In Brazil, giant specimens of rock crystal (quartz)
have been found that are as big as a child.
```

- **Many rocks**, especially igneous rocks, are made of crystals of different minerals.
- **Some crystals** are transparent and allow light to pass completely through them.
- **The way the atoms** of a crystal are arranged may allow the crystal to break along a flat surface. This is called mineral cleavage.
- **Some crystals** break with a rough surface. This is known as mineral fracture.

▲ *Rhodochrosite often forms in banded masses.*
This specimen shows flat, tabular crystals.

Other mineral shapes

- **The actual shape** in which a mineral forms is called its habit. This may be a perfect crystal shape or one of a number of other shapes.

- **Mineral habit** is a useful aid to help in identifying minerals.

- **When a mineral** forms no definite shape, it is said to have a massive habit. Lots of minerals, such as quartz and limonite (an iron mineral), have this habit. They can also be crystalline.

- **Rounded habits** are common. Hematite (iron oxide) often occurs as reniform (kidney-shaped) masses.

- **A botryoidal habit** is like a bunch of grapes, with many small, rounded structures. Malachite can occur like this.

- **Native metallic elements**, such as silver and copper, frequently form as wires. These can look like tree branches and this habit is called dendritic (from the Greek word for a tree).

- **Minerals** sometimes form in elongated masses like stalactites. Goethite (an iron mineral) often has this stalactitic habit.

- **Well-formed crystals** that have a constant shape in cross-section are said to possess prismatic habit. A hexagonal quartz crystal is prismatic.

◄ *Marcasite has the same chemical composition as pyrite, but has different forms. This marcasite 'sun' is a typical habit of the mineral.*

▶ *Native copper commonly occurs as twisted masses and wires.*

Mica crystals are flat and flaky, rather like a table top. This habit is called tabular.

A habit that looks like a fossil coral is called coralloidal. Aragonite (a form of calcium carbonate) sometimes occurs in this way.

▼ *This is not a fossil plant but delicate patterns formed by the mineral pyrolusite. This is known as a dendritic habit.*

Minerals in rocks

▶ *Feldspar is one of the most common rock-forming minerals. Orthoclase feldspar is often pink in colour.*

- **Minerals** are everywhere. All rocks contain minerals and many minerals form as magma or lava cools to make igneous rocks.

- **The elements** in the Earth's crust combine to make minerals, but only eight elements are very common, and these account for over 90 percent of the crust.

- **The main mineral-forming** elements are oxygen, silicon, aluminium, iron, calcium, sodium, potassium and magnesium.

- **Oxygen and silicon** are very important rock-forming elements, as together they are the basis of the 'family' of silicate minerals.

- **As magma or lava cools**, silicate minerals form in a definite sequence. The dense, heavy minerals that crystallize at the highest temperatures form first.

- **Olivine** is usually the first mineral to form, followed by pyroxene and amphibole. Feldspars, micas and quartz also crystallize in igneous rocks.

- **Many sedimentary rocks** contain minerals that have been eroded from other rocks. Limestone, however, contains calcite, which is formed for the first time in that rock.

....FASCINATING FACT....
Some recently discovered minerals form in
shipwrecks. Others form in blast furnace slag.

Metamorphic rocks have a number of special minerals in them. These
include garnet, kyanite and mica.

Certain minerals capitallize at low temperature on the Earth's crust.
A group called 'evaporites' (which includes halite and gypsum) form as
sea water dries.

▼ *As an igneous rock cools, minerals crystallize. In this basalt lava, olivine,
pyroxene and feldspar will be forming as the molten rock solidifies.*

Mineral occurrenc

- **Many of the finest mineral specimens** and some of the rarest minerals are found in mineral veins.

- **When rocks break** because of tension in the Earth's crust, faults and joints are formed. Hot fluids from great depths seep upwards into these cracks and deposit minerals. These fractures become mineral veins.

- **Hot mineral-forming fluids** are called hydrothermal fluids because they are rich in water.

- **Minerals** containing important metals such as galena (lead,) sphalerite (zinc), chalcopyrite (copper) and cassiterite (tin) occur in mineral veins.

- **Other common** hydrothermal vein minerals are fluorite, calcite and quartz.

- **Hydrothermal veins** are often associated with large granite batholiths. Hot mineral-rich fluids may form after much of the magma has cooled.

- **Granite** is a rock through which heat rises for millions of years after it has crystallized. Fluids from elsewhere in the Earth's crust may be drawn upwards by this heat and many deposit minerals near the granite.

- **A mineral vein** looks like a gash running through rocks. It is often white, containing quartz as the most common mineral.

- **Many minerals occur** in what are called placer deposits. These are concentrations of certain minerals in river sand and silt, especially where the water slows down on the inside of a meander or below rapids.

- **Only minerals** that are very durable and heavy are found in placers. Gold, tin, platinum and diamonds occur in placers.

▶ *A specimen of blue plumbogummite and yellowish pyromorphi Countless tonnes of economically useful minerals come from veins.*

Quartz

- **Quartz** is one of the most common minerals. It is widespread and occurs in most rocks.

- **Quartz** can be a great variety of colours. Some of the colour forms are semi-precious gemstones. Amethyst (purple), rose quartz (pink), smoky quartz (black and dark brown) and citrine (orange) are all cut and polished for jewellery.

- **Quartz** is the hardest common mineral. It is the defining mineral at point 7 on the hardness scale, and can't be scratched with a knife blade.

- **Agate**, a semi-precious stone formed in concentric bands, has the same chemical composition as quartz.

- **Chalcedony** is a variety of quartz made of microscopic crystals.

▲ *Amethyst is the purple-colour semi-precious form of quartz.*

··· FASCINATING FACT ···
The largest quartz crystal ever discovered was found in Brazil. It was 6 m long and weighed 48 tonnes.

Quartz often occurs as magnificent crystals. These are six-sided (hexagonal) and usually have six triangular faces, forming a pyramid at the top.

Quartz is made of atoms of silicon and oxygen in the form of silicon dioxide.

There are many ways in which quartz is used. Small crystals of quartz are used in the mechanisms of watches and electronics equipment.

Colourless, transparent quartz is called rock crystal.

▶ *This is a hexagonal crystal of smoky quartz (Cairngorm). It is translucent and light is able to penetrate the crystal.*

175

Cuprite and zincite

- **These two minerals** are metal ores. Cuprite is an oxide of copper, and zincite is zinc oxide.

- **Cuprite is rich-red** in colour. It is sometimes fashioned as a translucent gemstone, although it is rather soft.

- **When it is exposed** to strong light, the glassy surface may become dull.

- **This copper mineral** can form cube-shaped crystals and also eight- and twelve-sided crystals.

- **With a hardness of 4**, cuprite is slightly harder than a coin, but can be easily scratched by a steel knife blade.

- **Cuprite is an economically useful ore** of copper.

- **Zincite rarely occurs** as crystals. Usually it forms as irregular masses or grains.

- **Usually a red-coloured mineral**, zincite can also be orange or yellow.

- **Zincite is slightly harder** than cuprite at 4½, but is a little less dense. Cuprite has a density of 6.14 and zincite's density is 5.68.

- **Forming in the altered zones** of copper deposits, cuprite is a common mineral, but zincite is rarer, and fine specimens are prized by collectors.

▶ *In this specimen, cuprite forms small, bright-red crystals, which cover much of the rock surface. The white crystals are quartz.*

Spinel and rutile

▲ *These worn spinel crystals are from river gravel in Burma. Because it is hard and resitant to erosion by running water, this mineral often occurs in river sediments.*

Oxides are composed of metals combined with oxygen. Spinel is an oxide of magnesium and aluminium and metals such as zinc, manganese and iron. Rutile is an oxide of titanium dioxide.

Spinel forms as octahedra. These are crystals with eight triangular faces, which form two four-sided pyramids joined at their bases.

It has a great variety of colours and may be red, green, brown, black or blue.

It can be produced artificially, and these spinel specimens are slightly denser than natural ones.

It is an extremely hard mineral, registering nearly 8 on the hardness scale.

Spinel has been cut as a gemstone, prized for its colour and hardness.

Rutile often occurs as thin, needle-like crystals enclosed inside quartz crystals. It may also form as irregular masses.

It is dark in colour, varying from red-brown to black.

It is not as hard as spinel, having a hardness of 6 to $6\frac{1}{2}$.

...FASCINATING FACT...
Rutile is an important source of titanium, which is used
in lightweight alloys in aircraft and artificial hip joints.

Pyrolusite and chrysoberyl

- **The mineral pyrolusite** often occurs as strange, plantlike markings on rock surfaces. This is called a dendritic habit.

- **It can also form** as irregular masses, fibres and column-shaped specimens.

- **Pyrolusite** is an oxide of manganese, and is a black-coloured mineral, which can leave a dark powder when handled.

- **This mineral is found** in a variety of situations. It occurs in rounded nodules formed on the deep ocean bed, and in the altered parts of manganese veins.

- **It is a relatively dense mineral** – five times denser than water. Its hardness varies with its form, and can be as low as 2 or as high as 6½.

Chrysoberyl is an oxide of beryllium and aluminium. It is extremely hard (8½) and is often used as a gemstone.

- **Its colour varies** from green, to yellow and grey. The green form, called alexandrite, is the most common gem variety.

- **Other features** that increase its value as a gemstone are its glassy lustre and transparency.

- **It forms in igneous rocks**, especially pegmatites, and in metamorphic schists and marbles.

- **Chrysoberyl is so hard** that it can withstand weathering and erosion, and grains accumulate in sands deposited by rivers.

◄ *This specimen shows a number of twinned chrysoberyl crystals radiating away from each other.*

Goethite

▲ *Goethite often occurs in masses of small rounded aggregates. In this example these can be seen in the lower left and upper centre of the photograph.*

This mineral is named after the German writer Johann Wolfgang von Goethe (1749–1832), who was a mineral collector.

Goethite is rich in iron, and is mined as an ore of this metal. Chemically it is iron hydroxide.

It is a dark-coloured mineral. It can be black, dark brown or yellowish brown.

The yellowish-coloured material called limonite contains a lot of goethite. Some geologists regard limonite as a rock rather than a mineral because it contains various minerals.

It can form fine crystals, but more frequently goethite occurs as rounded or irregular specimens.

This is a relatively hard mineral – about the same as a knife blade at 5 to 5½.

As it contains iron, goethite is a dense mineral and specimens feel heavier than expected. Its density can be 4.3 times greater than that of water.

When light falls on its surface, goethite has a different appearance depending on its shape. Crystals reflect the light with a sparkling sheen called an adamantine lustre. Irregular specimens can look dull, with no sheen.

Goethite occurs where iron-bearing deposits have been altered by oxidation and weathering.

...FASCINATING FACT...
When heated, under certain conditions, goethite becomes magnetic.

Feldspar and mica

- **The group of minerals** called feldspars are the most common minerals in the Earth's crust. Feldspars are generally pale-coloured, though some are reddish, bluish or green.

- **Feldspar** makes up nearly half the composition of basalt lava, which covers the floor of the oceans.

- **Feldspar** is a silicate mineral containing silicon and oxygen. Different types of feldspar have atoms of different metallic elements.

- **Orthoclase feldspar** is a silicate of potassium and aluminium. This is common in granite.

◄ *This glittery mass of mica has typically thin, flaky crystals. Pale-coloured mica is called muscovite.*

▶ *Feldspar is a very common mineral and is commonly white or pale-coloured. Amazonite is a brilliant blue-green variety, seen here as fine crystals.*

Plagioclase feldspar has a variable composition. It is a silicate of sodium and aluminium or calcium and aluminium. This feldspar mainly occurs in basalt and related rocks.

Feldspar is used in pottery glazes and glass. It alters to china clay when decomposed.

Mica is a complex silicate containing potassium, aluminium and iron.

Because of its very glittery appearance and flaky habit, mica is easy to identify.

Mica is common in many igneous rocks, especially granite.

Mica has good insulating properties and is often powdered and used for this purpose.

Augite and hornblende

- **A member of the mineral group** called pyroxenes, augite is a silicate formed at high temperatures in magma and lava.

- **Augite is a dark**, virtually black mineral that helps to give basic rocks their dark colouring. It can also be brown or dark green.

- **Augite crystals** are small, prismatic and stubby.

- **Augite crystals** make up about 50 percent of gabbro, a coarse-grained igneous rock.

- **Hornblende** is very like augite in appearance. It belongs to the amphibole group of minerals.

- **A very dark-coloured** mineral, hornblende can be green, brown or black.

- **The crystals** formed by hornblende are long and prismatic, often with a fibrous appearance.

- **Hornblende forms** in pale-coloured igneous rocks such as granite and porphyry.

- **The metamorphic rock** called amphibolite contains much hornblende.

- **When hornblende and augite break**, different angles are produced between the cleavage. Hornblende breaks with an angle of either 60° or 120° between them. Augite breaks with 90° between the surfaces.

▶ *Hornblende and augite can be difficult to tell apart.*
This hornblende crystal is more slender than typical augite crystals.

▲ *Augite crystals tend to be short and stubby.*
When they break, rectangular shapes are formed,
s in the large specimen on the left.

187

Olivine

- **Olivine crystallizes** at very high temperatures in basalts and related rocks.

- **It is a greenish** or brown mineral, which occurs as small grains or crystals.

- **The colour of olivine** varies depending on its chemical composition. It is a silicate of iron and magnesium. An increase in iron content gives a browner colour.

- **One of the hardest** rock-forming minerals, olivine is almost as hard as quartz.

- **Meteorites** found in Antarctica, belonging to a group called 'stony-irons', are made of metal and the mineral olivine.

- **Because of its green colour** and hardness, fine crystalline olivine is used as a gemstone called peridot.

- **Gem-quality olivine** comes mainly from Arizona, USA, Myanmar (Burma) and Norway.

- **In basalt lava**, olivine occurs as bright green, rounded crystals studding the rock surface.

- **Peridotite**, a rock which forms very deep in the Earth's crust, is composed of garnet and olivine.

- **Dunite** is an igneous rock made almost entirely of olivine. It has a greenish-brown appearance.

▶ *In this specimen of basalt from Hawaii, there is a mass of pale green olivine crystals.*

Olivine can be cut and facetted as a gem stone. This small cut stone is surrounded by water-worn olivine crystals. Gem quality olivine is called peridot.

Hemimorphite and epidote

◀ *This specimen of hemimorphite, from a mineral vein, consists of a number of small transparent crystals.*

- **The mineral hemimorphite** is a hydrated zinc silicate, and epidote is a silicate of calcium, aluminium and iron.

- **It has a wide range of colours** and shapes. It can be a striking blue, grey, green, yellow or whitish colour.

- **The shape of hemimorphite varies** from rounded masses to thin, squat crystals.

- **Hemimorphite is harder than a coin**, but with a hardness of 4½, it can be scratched with a steel knife blade.

- **It forms where lead and zinc** deposits have been altered with other minerals, such as cerussite, sphalerite and galena.
- **Epidote is a dark-green**, grey or almost black mineral, which may be transparent. The crystal faces have a glassy sheen.
- **This mineral commonly forms** as well-shaped crystals, which have thin, lengthwise grooves (striations) on their faces.
- **It is a hard mineral.** At 6 to 7, it cannot be marked by a steel knife blade.
- **Epidote has a density of 3.4 to 3.5**, which is just above average for materials in the Earth's crust.
- **This mineral forms** in metamorphic and igneous rocks.

▼ *A perfect, dark-coloured epidote crystal, showing its striated surfaces and vitreous (glassy) lustre.*

Dioptase and spodumene

- **A very beautiful and collectable mineral,** dioptase is a hydrous copper silicate.

- **It has a striking, rich, emerald-green colour,** and the crystal faces have a glassy sheen.

- **Dioptase forms** as masses of short crystals, which may be transparent.

- **With a hardness of 5,** dioptase is harder than a coin, but can be marked by a steel knife blade.

- **It occurs where veins** containing copper have been altered. It is associated with other minerals, including wulfenite, chrysocolla and cerussite.

- **Spodumene is a lithium aluminium silicate** and is an important source of the element lithium.

- **Lithium is the lightest metal** and has a variety of industrial applications in glass and batteries.

- **The green form** of spodumene is called hiddenite, and the pink variety is kunzite. It can also be white or grey in colour.

- **The crystals of spodumene** are transparent, and their surfaces are harder than a knife blade, with a hardness of $6\frac{1}{2}$ to $7\frac{1}{2}$.

- **This mineral occurs in granite** and coarse-grained granitic rocks called pegmatites.

◀ *This specimen shows a dark, green-coloured dioptase and pale quartz growing together among the rock debris in a mineral vein.*

Actinolite and riebeckite

- **The mineral actinolite** is a complex silicate mineral that contains the metal calcium, magnesium and iron.

- **It belongs to the family of minerals** called amphiboles. These are common in many igneous and metamorphic rocks.

- **This mineral is usually dark in colour** – dark green to almost black. However, scratches on the surface are white.

- **It is relatively hard** at 5 to 6, and may be marked by a steel knife blade.

- **It occurs mainly** in metamorphic rocks, especially schist and amphibolite.

- **Another complex silicate**, riebeckite forms as long, thin crystals.

- **This mineral is dark blue** to black in colour, and the crystal surfaces have a silky sheen.

- **With a hardness of 5**, it can be scratched with a steel knife blade.

- **Fibrous riebeckite** (crocidolite) has asbestos-like properties, which is why it is known as 'blue asbestos'. It has been used for heat and electrical insulation

···**FASCINATING FACT**···
Actinolite crystals are long and narrow, and often form in clusters.
They are so slender that they can easily be bent.

▲ *This riebeckite shows a silky lustre. It is composed of many slender, fibrous crystals This form is known as crocidolite.*

Talc and kaolinite

- **One of the softest minerals** to be found is talc. It is used to define hardness on the hardness scale. It feels greasy, and rubs off on the hands.

- **This mineral is a hydrous silicate** of magnesium, and forms by the alteration of ultra-basic igneous rocks and dolomite limestones.

- **Talc rarely occurs** as thin, flat crystals. More often it forms as irregular masses or fibrous aggregates.

- **Its colour is white**, grey or greenish, and is marked white when scratched.

- **It is of average density** – 2.6 to 2.8 times denser than water.

- **Talc has a number of industrial uses** and is important in the manufacture of paper, rubber and cosmetics and being processed into the form we know as talcum powder.

Kaolinite is a hydrous silicate of aluminium, formed by the alteration of feldspars in igneous rocks.

The name kaolinite refers to a group of 'clay' minerals.

It rarely occurs as crystals, more commonly as irregular masses.

This is a soft mineral at 2 to 2½ in hardness and its density is 2.2 to 2.7.

● **Kaolinite is the main constituent** of kaolin or china clay and is of great importance in paper production, toothpaste, medicines and the ceramics industry.

◀ *This specimen of pink and white kaolinite has no obvious crystals. The term 'massive' is used to describe a mineral with no crystal form.*

Galena and cassiterite

▶ *Galena is a heavy, metallic, lead-grey mineral. It occurs in mineral veins with quartz, fluorite and calcite.*

- **Galena** (lead sulphide) has been mined since Roman times as an ore of lead.

- **A very dense mineral**, galena is made of lead sulphide, and is 7.5 times heavier than an equal volume of water.

- **Galena** is a soft, grey-coloured mineral, easily scratched with a coin. It crystallizes in the cubic system and is often found as near perfect cubes.

- **Lead** was once used to make water and gas pipes because it was easily bent to the correct shape. However, it fractures, and produces a cumulative poison that builds up in the body.

▶ *Cassiterite is an important ore of tin, which occurs in veins.*

For thousands of years the county of Cornwall in the UK was a source of tin, extracted from cassiterite (tin oxide).

This mineral occurs in hydrothermal veins, often associated with large granite batholiths.

Cassiterite can be recognized by its dark brown or black colour and high density. It is a hard mineral – even a knife blade will not scratch it.

About 5000 years ago, the Mesopotamians made bronze by adding tin to copper.

Pewter, used much in the past for drinking vessels, is an alloy of tin and lead. Tin is used today in solder and tin plate.

● **Today lead is used** in vehicle batteries and as a shield against radioactive sources.

◀ *Today, one of the main uses of lead is for the plates in vehicle batteries. Lead is obtained from galena.*

Chalcocite and bornite

- **These two minerals** are common sulphides of copper. Bornite also contains iron.

- **Both chalcocite and bornite** are important ores that are mined for their copper content.

- **Chalcocite forms** in the same mineral veins as bornite, along with other minerals such as galena and sphalerite.

- **It rarely forms crystals**. It usually occurs as shapeless masses.

- **It is a dark-grey mineral**, and shines like metal when light falls on its surface

- **A soft mineral**, chalcocite can be easily scratched by a coin, having a hardne of 2½ to 3.

- **Bornite forms in fine**, cube-shaped crystals, and also in eight- or twelve-sided crystals.

- **This mineral can be a variety of colours**, indicating its copper and iron content. It can be copper-red, bronze or brown.

- **For an ore of a metal**, bornite is a soft mineral, and can be marked by a coin Its hardness is 3.

...**FASCINATING FACT**...
Bornite is named after the Austrian geologist
Ignaz Edler von Born (1745–1791).

▲ *This specimen has some pale masses of quartz among the purple-tarnished bornite. It is from Cumbria, UK, where, many years ago, copper was mined.*

Cinnabar

- **This mineral** is bright red or occasionally a brownish colour.

- **It forms around volcanic craters** and hot springs, and in fractures in sedimentary rocks.

- **Cinnabar is usually found** as shapeless masses, but it can form as fine, six-sided crystals.

- **It is a soft mineral** that is easily marked by a coin.

- **It occurs with other minerals,** including pyrite, realgar, quartz and calcite.

- **Cinnabar is the main source** of the metal mercury, which is extracted by heating.

- **Mercury is a poisonous metal,** and cinnabar should be handled with care.

- **It is heavy and dense** at more than eight times as dense as water.

- **Mercury is a heavy liquid** at ordinary temperatures, and has been used in thermometers and dental fillings.

- **As well as occurring in cinnabar,** mercury is widespread throughout the natural world found in corderoite and other minerals but poisonous to most animals and plants.

◄ *Cinnabar can form as six-sided crystals, but is usually found as irregular masses, as is shown in this picture.*

Stibnite and cobaltite

- **These two minerals** are both sulphides. Stibnite contains antimony and cobaltite contains cobalt, arsenic and iron.

- **Stibnite often forms** in long, thin crystals that sometimes radiate out from a rock surface.

- **It is dark grey in colour** with a metallic sheen.

- **It is very soft** and as its hardness is only 2, it can be scratched with a fingernail.

- **Its density** is just over $4\frac{1}{2}$ times greater than that of water.

- **It is an important ore mineral**, and is the main source of the metal antimony. This is used mainly for adding to other metals to make them harder.

- **Cobaltite forms in crystals** that have grooves on their faces. It can also occur as grains and irregular masses.

- **The colour varies**, but usually it is silvery grey with a metallic sheen.

- **It has a hardness** of $5\frac{1}{2}$. It cannot be marked by a knife blade, but a specimen of quartz will scratch it.

- **Cobaltite is an important ore of cobalt**, a silvery metal. Like iron, cobaltite can be magnetized, and is used to make magnets. It is also used in paint and pottery. Radioactive cobalt-60 is important in medical treatment.

▼ *This small crystal of cobaltite shows the typical silvery-grey colouring. Cobaltite occurs in mineral veins in many parts of the world.*

Arsenopyrite and marcasite

▼ *This elongated mass of globular marcasit is from the chalk of southern England. Marcasite is often found in sedimentary rocks.*

The mineral arsenopyrite is a sulphide of iron and arsenic. Marcasite is a form of iron sulphide.

Arsenopyrite occurs as elongated crystals, and also as grains and irregular masses.

It is a relatively hard mineral, about the same hardness as a steel knife blade. Its density is around six times that of water.

This mineral is silvery-grey in colour, but tarnishes to brown and pink.

Arsenic can be sourced from arsenopyrite, and the use of this poisonous element is controlled.

It forms in mineral veins with other minerals including quartz and calcite, and in silver- and gold-bearing deposits.

- **Pyrite is chemically the same** as marcasite, but the crystal forms of the two are very different.

- **This form of iron sulphide** occurs in a variety of shapes, often with curved crystal faces. Nodules (rounded lumps) of marcasite have radiating internal structures.

- **It is paler in colour** than pyrite and is brassy yellow, but gets darker after prolonged exposure in the atmosphere.

...FASCINATING FACT...
When arsenopyrite is struck
with a hard object, a smell
of garlic is produced.

Molybdenite

▲ *Molybdenite (1) often forms on fractured surfaces in granite. These silvery flakes are from granite at Shap in Cumbria, UK. Also in the picture are small, golden crystals of pyrite (2).*

This chemical compound has two atoms of sulphur combining with every one of molybdenum. It is a sulphide of the element molybdenum.

It is easy to recognize by its appearance and other properties. It crystallizes in flat, six-sided plates and tapering crystals.

Molybdenite has a silvery-grey colour, and shines like metal.

A silvery-grey powder (the mineral's streak) is left on the hands when the mineral is touched.

It is a very soft mineral, and can even be scratched with a fingernail.

The density of molybdenite is nearly five times that of water.

It occurs in mineral veins with quartz and cassiterite, and also in granite, where it forms as silvery coatings on joint surfaces.

This mineral is the main ore of the metal molybdenum.

Molybdenum has a variety of important uses. It is used in alloys with other metals and in electrodes.

Molybdenite has a greasy feel, and this is related to its use as an additive in lubricants.

Iron ores

- **Iron** is one of the most sought-after raw materials.

- **Many** of the sedimentary iron ores of the Jurassic Age in England are now composed of rusty coloured limonite. This resulted from the weathering of other iron minerals and concentrated the iron into sufficient quantities to make it workable. In the fresh state, many of these ores were not economic to work.

- **Most iron ore** mined today is found in sedimentary rocks. The richest deposits are in Labrador (Canada,) Hamersley (Western Australia,) near Lake Superior (USA), and in the Ukraine.

- **Hematite (iron oxide)** is a rich ore. It is a mineral with either a black or a reddish colour.

- **Hematite** frequently occurs in rounded, 'kidney ore' shapes. The crystalline form is called specularite.

- **As it contains iron**, hematite is a heavy mineral with a specific gravity 5.26 times heavier than water.

▶ *This 2000-year-old iron chain was found in a Welsh Lake called Llyn Cerrig Bach.*

▶ *Two different varieties of hematite are seen in this specimen – reddish, rounded kidney ore and black, crystalline specularite.*

Magnetite is another rich source of iron. This oxide of iron forms as black crystals or massive, irregular specimens.

As its name suggests, magnetite is magnetic. This magnetism is strong enough to move a compass needle and attract iron filings.

Mountaineers and walkers in areas where the rocks contain magnetite will find their compasses give inaccurate readings.

Magnetite is a hard mineral and can't be scratched by a knife blade.

In Tenerife in the Canary Islands, there are black magnetite sand beaches, made of iron ore that has been weathered out of lava.

Bauxite

- **Some geologists** argue that bauxite is a rock, not a mineral, because it is a mixture of various materials. These include several oxides of aluminium.

- **Bauxite is usually formed** by the weathering of other rocks rich in silicates of aluminium. This happens mainly in tropical regions.

- **It is an attractive material**, being orange or buff-coloured and containing red specks and patches.

- **As well as aluminium**, bauxite commonly contains some iron oxide.

▼ *Bauxite is a dull, red-brown ore of aluminium. This is the most abundant of all metals and much electrical energy is needed to extract it from bauxite.*

▶ *Aluminium is very strong and lightweight. Unlike steel it does not rust, so it is suitable for aircraft construction. This Boeing 747 is made from many tonnes of aluminium.*

Bauxite is a very soft material, easily scratched with a fingernail. It is also low density and is only 2.5 times heavier than water.

Much mined for its aluminium content, bauxite is the major source of this metal.

Aluminium conducts electricity well and is lightweight.

It is obtained from its ore by electrolysis. This involves the use of much electricity, which is often low-cost hydroelectricity.

Aluminium is very resistant to corrosion. It does not rust like iron and steel.

Because of its strength and light weight, aluminium is used in the construction industry and increasingly in vehicle manufacture.

Diamond and graphite

◀ *Diamond has been prized as a gemstone for thousands of years. This example has been cut and facetted to show off its sparkle.*

- **Diamond and graphite** are remarkably different forms of the same element, carbon. The properties of these two forms of carbon result from the way their atoms are joined.

- **Many diamonds** may be over 3000 million years old.

- **Graphite** is very soft, being easily scratched with a fingernail.

- **Diamond** forms small, glassy, often octahedral crystals in the cubic crystal system and is the hardest known mineral.

- **Graphite** forms in flat, platelike pieces with a six-sided outline (hexagonal crystal system). These have a dull, greasy or metallic sheen.

- **The atoms in diamond** are joined in groups of five. These link together in a tight, close structure.

- **In graphite**, the atoms are arranged in layers or sheets that are weakly joined.

▲ *Diamonds occur in a rock called kimberlite. Two small diamond crystals are in this kimberlite from South Africa.*

Diamond is much prized as a gemstone and is also used for industrial cutting.

Graphite is used as pencil 'lead'. The pencil industry in Keswick, UK, was based on local graphite.

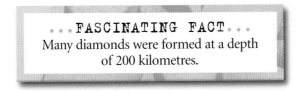

...FASCINATING FACT...
Many diamonds were formed at a depth
of 200 kilometres.

Birthstones

- **For nearly 2000 years**, crystals and precious stones have been linked with months of the year. Different religious and cultural groups have associated different stones with the months. The associations shown here are those popular in western culture today.

- **Garnet**, a gemstone often with a rich, dark red colour, and found in metamorphic rocks, is the birthstone for January.

- **The birthstone for February** is amethyst. This is a purple, semi-precious form of quartz.

- **If you are born in March** or May, forms of beryl are your birthstones. March is represented by pale blue aquamarine and May by green emerald.

- **The most valued gemstone**, diamond, is the birthstone for April.

- **June** has an organic gemstone, pearl, as its birthstone.

- **Ruby**, the birthstone for July, and sapphire, September's birthstone, are both forms of corundum, the second-hardest mineral.

- **A gem variety** of the silicate mineral olivine, called peridot, represents the month of August.

- **Opal**, a gemstone with a rich play of colours, which can change as the stone is heated, is the birthstone for October.

- **The third-hardest gemstone**, topaz, is the birthstone for people born in November. Turquoise, a rich blue gemstone, is linked with December.

▶ *Each month of the year is characterized by a certain gemstone. The exact stones representing each month have not always been the same and those used in certain countries are different. The stones here are those generally used today.*

December
Turquoise

January
Garnet

November
Topaz

February
Amethyst

October
Opal

March
Aquamarine

September
Sapphire

April
Diamond

August
Peridot

May
Emerald

July
Ruby

June
Pearl

Beryl and tourmaline

- **These two minerals** are both silicates of various metals. They occur in igneous rocks such as granites and pegmatites.

- **Beryl** is harder than quartz and forms fine, hexagonal crystals.

- **A number** of colour varieties of beryl are known, many of which are gemstones. Emerald is the rich green variety of beryl, heliodor is yellow, morganite is a pink form and aquamarine is greenish-blue.

- **Beryl can be translucent** or transparent, and has a glassy lustre (sheen).

- **Tourmaline** is not uncommon in granites, where it forms black prismatic crystals. This type of tourmaline is called schorl.

- **With a hardness of 7**, tourmaline is as hard as quartz. It forms prismatic crystals and may be transparent.

- **There are more** colour varieties of tourmaline than of any other gemstone.

▶ *Some of the colour varieties of tourmaline.*

▲ *A fine prismatic crystal of beryl in pegmatite. This green-coloured beryl is called emerald and it is used as a gemstone.*

Rubellite is pink tourmaline, and the green form is called elbaite. It can also be blue, yellowish and grey-blue.

Some tourmaline crystals are green at one end and pink at the other.

> ...FASCINATING FACT...
> The largest crystal ever found was a beryl crystal discovered in Madagascar in 1976. It was 18 m long and weighed 380 tonnes.

Opal

- **Opal** is a form of silicon dioxide, but is chemically different from quartz because it also contains water in its structure.

- **The silica** in opal is packed together in minute spheres. Opal is thus a non-crystalline mineral.

- **Opal** occurs in many different forms. It can be botryoidal (shaped like a bunch of grapes), reniform (kidney-shaped) or shaped like a stalactite.

- **Opal** is a well-known gemstone, though it is not of great hardness. Nevertheless, it has a number of attractive features.

- **Because of the packing** of minute spheres in the structure of opal, light is scattered to produce many colours. These vary from blue and green to red and pink. When heated, opal may change colour.

- **Another feature** of gem opal is the way it produces flashes of colour, which are best shown in curved, polished specimens called cabochons.

- **Opal** forms in certain volcanic rocks, but also often around hot springs.

- **The Romans** considered opal to be a symbol of power and the Aztec civilization valued it as a gem.

- **Today**, much of the world's opal comes from Australia, but some also comes from Mexico.

...FASCINATING FACT...
Fossilized trees are sometimes made of wood opal.
This replaces the woody tissue perfectly.

This Australian opal shows typical colour variation from green to blue. Being translucent, light passes into the mineral and gives the colours depth.

Geodes and agates

- **A geode** is a gas cavity (vesicle) in lava, usually basalt, which has been filled in with minerals. Quartz in various forms is common in geodes.

- **Basalt lava** erupts onto the Earth's surface at over 1000°C. As it cools, gas is released and small cavities are left where the gas bubbles were trapped.

- **When basalt** containing geodes is weathered, the geodes, being very hard, are left behind. They often look like lumpy potatoes, but when cut open the wonderful coloured bands of agate are revealed.

- **In some geodes**, agate lines the cavity and delicate crystals grow into the hollow interior.

- **Agate** is not made of crystalline quartz. In an agate, the quartz is in minute fibres and grains.

▼ *A true geode has a hollow in its centre with crystals growing into it. This specimen h been nearly all infilled with quartz. There is a thin band of agate around the outer edg*

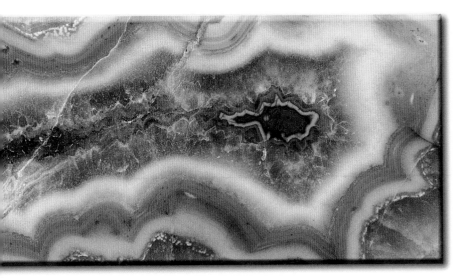

▲ *This agate shows typical alternating colour bands.*
The specimen has been cut and polished.

Agate is one of the most varied semi-precious stones. It occurs in many forms and colours.

A hard gemstone, agate is translucent, and can be grey, blue, red, green, white or other colours.

Agate often occurs in bands of different colours. These may be parallel (onyx) or concentric.

South American agates from Uruguay and Brazil are the most common.

In Britain, agates can be found in many places. Southern Scotland is the source of the best British agates. They also occur in the Cheviot Hills in Northumberland, in Cornwall and on North Sea beaches.

Native raw element

- **As well as gold and diamond**, there are a number of other minerals that are important native elements.

- **Copper** is a metal that occurs as dendritic and shapeless, massive specimens. It is soft and easily scratched, but is very dense.

- **Copper** also combines with other elements in various minerals. One of its main uses is in electrical wiring.

- **Arsenic** usually occurs as rounded, botryoidal masses and can also be found in the form of grains.

- **A group of minerals** called arsenates contain arsenic combined with other elements. Arsenic is poisonous.

- **Sulphur** is a bright yellow element that can occur as fine pyramidal crystals

- **Sulphur** forms around hot springs and volcanic craters. It often combines with other elements to form the sulphide group of minerals.

- **The element bismuth**, a silvery, metallic mineral that is soft but very dense, occurs in hydrothermal veins and pegmatites.

- **Bismuth** also occurs combined with sulphur as a mineral called bismuthinite.

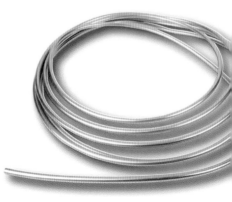

▶ *Native copper is used to make copper wire. This is a good conductor of electricity.*

▲ *Sulphur's crystals are clearly visible and are a bright yellow colour. This specimen is from Mexico. Sulphur has important industrial uses, especially in the manufacture of sulphuric acid.*

...FASCINATING FACT...
Copper pins and beads have been discovered in the
Middle East, dating back more than 7000 years.

Radioactive minerals

- **There are a few minerals** that contain uranium, a dense, radioactive element.

- **Uranium** combines with oxygen to form uraninite (pitchblende), with copper, phosphorus and oxygen to form torbernite. It also combines with calcium, phosphorus and oxygen to make autunite.

- **Uranium** is sought after as a source of fuel for nuclear reactors. Other highly radioactive elements, such as plutonium, can be made from it.

- **Uraninite**, or pitchblende, occurs as cube-shaped crystals or in rounded masses. A very dense mineral, uraninite is up to ten times heavier than water.

- **Torbernite** forms as bright green, box-shaped crystals. These have a shiny surface.

- **Easily scratched** with a coin, torbernite forms by the alteration of uraninite by fluids in the Earth's crust.

- **Autunite** is bright yellow or green and occurs as small crystals and crusty masses.

...FASCINATING FACT...

In 1898 the Polish scientist Marie Curie and her French husband Pierre discovered radioactivity. They identified the elements radium, potassium and helium in a specimen of pitchblende, a variety of uraninite. Radium from pitchblende is widely used in medicine and industry.

Like torbernite autunite is easily scratched with a coin and is only of average density.

Radioactive minerals are only for expert use. They have to be stored securely, often in lead-lined containers.

Proton
Neutron
Electron

*By splitting
ɪnium atoms,
ɣh levels of energy
ɛ produced. The
ɔm's nucleus (centre),
ɪich makes up almost
 of its mass, is made up
protons and neutrons. These
ɛ held together by a very strong
rce. By harnessing this force, nuclear
ɛrgy is made.*

Toxic minerals

◀ *Paint pigments are often made from powdered minerals.*

● **Many minerals** are poisonous. The two described here, orpiment and realgar, are sulphides of arsenic and can be dangerous. Because of their remarkable colours, they have been used as pigment in paint.

● **Orpiment** is a wonderful golden yellow colour. Indeed, it is so golden that hundreds of years ago, alchemists tried to extract gold from it.

● **Orpiment** usually occurs in mineral veins and around hot springs. Like many arsenic minerals, it smells of garlic when heated.

● **It has** a resinous appearance and forms thin, flaky pieces or small crystals.

● **The yellow paint pigment** made from orpiment is called 'King's Yellow'.

● **Realgar** is found in the same geological situations as orpiment. It has a very similar chemical composition, but is a vivid red colour.

● **Realgar** has small, prismatic crystals, which often have lines on their surfaces.

● **The surface** of realgar has a greasy sheen. It is a very soft mineral, easily scratched with a fingernail.

● **Orpiment and realgar** are readily available from mineral dealers. They are not dangerous if carefully stored and if hands are well-washed after handling specimens.

● **Over 3500 years ago,** the Egyptians used crushed realgar as a paint pigment.

▶ *Reaglar is easily recognized by its rich red colouring and greasy sheen.*

◀ *Orpiment is usually a rich golden yellow colour. It occurs in mineral veins and around hot springs.*

Crocoite and wulfenite

- **Both these minerals are brightly coloured**, and they occur as fine crystals, which are sought by mineral collectors.

- **Crocoite is lead chromate**, a compound of lead, chromium and oxygen.

- **Its colour**, commonly bright red-orange, is crocoite's most striking property. The crystal surfaces shine like glass.

- **Crocoite forms** in thin, elongated crystals, which usually occur in masses on rock surfaces.

- **It is easily scratched** with a coin, and has a high density of 6 because of its lead content.

- **Crocoite occurs in lead veins** that have been altered by fluids containing chromium. Associated minerals include wulfenite and pyromorphite.

Wulfenite is usually a bright-yellow colour, with a glassy sheen. It can also be brown or green in colour.

This mineral is a compound of lead, molybdenum and oxygen, referred to as lead molybdate.

Like crocoite, wulfenite is easily scratched by a coin, but it is even more dense, being as much as seven times denser than water.

The first isolation of the element chromium was from crocoite.

◄ *These striking red crystals of crocoite are from Tasmania, where this mineral is found in lead-bearing veins that have been altered by oxidation.*

Adamite and erythrite

- **Both these minerals** are highly collectable, with bright colours and a variety of shapes.

- **Adamite is usually** bright green or yellow, with a glassy sheen.

- **It often occurs** as globular masses, but thin or flattened crystals are also found.

- **The mineral adamite** is a compound of zinc, arsenic, oxygen and hydrogen. This is called a hydrous zinc arsenate.

- **Because of its lead content**, this mineral has a high density – 4.4 times denser than water. It has the same hardness as a coin, 3½.

- **When placed** in dilute acids, adamite dissolves quickly.

- **Erythrite is purple-pink** or deep purple in colour, and may be transparent.

- **This mineral forms** as masses of thin, blade-shaped crystals.

- **Erythrite is a compound** of cobalt, arsenic, oxygen and water. It is classified as a hydrated cobalt arsenate.

···FASCINATING FACT···

Erythrite forms by the alteration of cobalt minerals, and so is a good clue for prospectors (people who look for places where there are mineral deposits or oil) as to where these deposits occur.

▼ *These crystal of erythrite show the brilliant pink and purple colours that indicate the presence of cobalt-bearing minerals.*

Pyromorphite and vanadinite

- **Both of these minerals** are sought by collectors.

- **Pyromorphite is commonly green** in colour, although it can also be brown, yellow or orange.

- **It occurs as short, stubby crystals**, which frequently look like small barrels.

- **It is made up of lead**, phosphorous, oxygen and chlorine. Its chemical name is lead phosphate chloride.

- **This chemical composition** gives the mineral a very high density of 6.5 to 7.1. It is slightly harder than a coin, at $3\frac{1}{2}$ to 4.

- **Pyromorphite** occurs in mineral veins containing lead, which have been altered by fluids seeping through them.

- **Vanadinite is often a grey** or rich, red colour, but it can also be orange or yellow.

- **It forms in small, six-sided crystals**, often as great masses. These crystals are occasionally hollow.

- **It is a dense mineral at 6.8 to 7**, and can be scratched with a coin, as its hardness is 3.

- **Vanadinite contains lead**, vanadium, chlorine and oxygen and is an ore of vanadium. This metal is used in steel, as it resists corrosion.

◄ *This typical specimen of vanadinite shows many small, six-sided crystals on a rock specimen from a mineral vein. It commonly occurs with lead minerals such as galena.*

Wavellite and turquoise

◄ *Because of its brilliant blue colouring, turquoise is often used ornamentally. These small specimens have been polished to show off their colours.*

- **Both these minerals have complex**, but similar, chemical compositions. Wavellite is a hydrated aluminium phosphate. Turquoise is a hydrated phosphate of copper and aluminium.

- **Wavellite is well-known** for its radiating crystal aggregates. These form in rounded masses, with an internal radiating structure.

- **This mineral varies in colour** from green to yellow, with a pearly or glassy sheen.

- **It is slightly harder than a coin**, at $3\frac{1}{2}$ to 4, and has a low density of 2.36.

- **It occurs in mineral veins** and on fractures in rocks that fluids have moved through.

- **Turquoise is known** for its decorative uses, in both jewellery and ornament

- **Its main feature** is its bright-blue colour. It may also be green or grey.

- **It usually occurs** as irregular masses and crusts on rock surfaces. It rarely forms as small crystals.

When rounded masses of wavellite
e broken, their internal structure of radiating crystals
n be seen. The specimen at the top left of the picture shows this well.

Another important feature in minerals that are used for jewellery is hardness. Although not of great hardness, turquoise resists some scratching at hardness 5 to 6.

Turquoise forms in rocks rich in aluminium that have been altered by ground water.

Fool's gold

- **There are a number** of minerals that on first sight have the appearance of gold. Small golden flecks of mineral in a stream bed may catch the eye but after testing are found not to be the real thing.

- **The two minerals** generally referred to as fool's gold are pyrite (iron sulphide) and chalcopyrite (copper iron sulphide).

- **With a few simple tests**, it is very easy to tell real gold from other minerals, and not be fooled.

- **Pyrite** is a common mineral in many geological situations. It occurs in mineral veins, metamorphic and sedimentary rocks, and in some igneous rocks. Fossils are often preserved in pyrite.

- **The true colour** of pyrite is silvery yellow, not a rich deep yellow.

- **Gold** is a very soft mineral, which can be scratched with a coin, but pyrite is harder than a knife blade.

- **Chalcopyrite** is a deeper yellow than pyrite and nearer to gold in colour. However, chalcopyrite tarnishes on exposure to air to give wonderful 'peacock' colours.

▶ *Pyrite commonly occurs as fine, cube-shaped crystals which, as shown here, have striations (lines) on their faces.*

Chalcopyrite is softer than pyrite, but harder than gold.

Both types of fool's gold are not nearly as dense as near true gold. An equal-sized specimen of gold would be far heavier than the impostors.

Chalcopyrite is a valuable mineral, being a very important ore of copper.

▶ *Chalcopyrite is a richer yellow colour than pyrite. It is also less hard and can be scratched with a knife blade.*

Healing crystals

- **For thousands of years** a number of minerals have been associated with medicine and healing. Minerals such as common quartz are still prized by many people for their healing properties.

- **Early civilizations**, including the Aztecs and Incas, used crystals for their supposed ability to heal.

- **Quartz** is thought to have great healing properties. This may stem from its ability to vibrate consistently. A perfect quartz crystal can allow meditation at a deep level.

- **Sapphire**, a form of corundum, is believed to be a healing mineral. It is supposedly good for backache and skin disorders. It may also help the spirit and promote contentment and peace of mind.

- **Opal** has had a mixed reception as a healing mineral. It is claimed to induce daydreaming, which may not be a good thing.

- **Tourmaline** is said to give confidence, relieve nervousness and promote self-assurance.

- **In Taos**, New Mexico, the Crystal Academy has been set up to promote the use of crystals in healing.

◀ *Sapphire is a form of corundum. It is believed to have healing and soothing properties.*

Topaz is thought to relieve high blood pressure and is also believed to cure insomnia.

Malachite, the bright green copper mineral, may relieve asthma and depression.

It is not known how crystal healing works. It may be related to light reflecting off the crystals having an effect on the body's electromagnetic field.

▶ *Quartz crystals are supposed to have many healing properties.*

Halite and gypsum

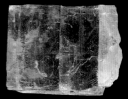

◀ *A specimen of slender gypsum crystals. This type of transparent gypsum is called selenite.*

▶ *Halite can form as cube-shaped crystals. These examples are transparent.*

These minerals are both evaporites, formed by the drying up of salt lakes and shallow seas. Halite is a chloride and gypsum a sulphate.

Both minerals are of considerable economic importance, being used in the chemical and construction industries.

Gypsum (hydrated calcium sulphate) is the basis for the manufacture of plaster and plasterboard. It is also used in cement manufacture.

Halite, (sodium chloride) is used in the manufacture of soap, dyes, caustic soda, insecticides and chlorine. It is also used for de-icing roads.

Large chemical industries are sited in England and Germany, where concentrations of salt (halite) occurs.

Halite can be readily identified by its salty taste. It is usually orange, grey or white in colour, but can be black.

Because it is very soluble, the cube-shaped crystals tend to lose their sharp edges unless they are kept in sealed, dry containers.

Halite is very soft, and easily scratched with a fingernail.

Gypsum often occurs as fine crystals. These can be diamond shaped or long and thin. A form called 'daisy gypsum' is like a rosette of tiny flowers.

Gypsum is the definition of point 2 on the minerals hardness scale.

◄ One of the uses of halite is in the manufacture of soap.

Atacamite and boleite

- **These two minerals** are classified as halides. This group contains minerals that are chemical compounds of halogen elements (chlorine, fluorine, bromine and iodine) and metals.

- **Both atacamite and boleite** have complex chemical formulae. Atacamite contains copper and chlorine, and boleite is made up of lead, silver, copper and chlorine.

- **Recognized by its green colouring**, atacamite varies from rich, dark green to pale green.

- **This mineral forms** as thin, elongated crystals, often in large masses on rock surfaces.

- **Atacamite is a soft mineral**, and can be scratched with a coin. It is 3.6 to 3. times denser than water.

- **Boleite forms as small, cube-shaped** crystals that are deep blue in colour.

- **This mineral is denser** than atacamite – five times as dense as water. Both minerals have the same hardness of 3 to 3½.

- **It occurs where lead deposits** have been altered by fluids running through them.

...**FASCINATING FACT**...
Atacamite is named after Atacama in Chile, South America,
a desert where it occurs around volcanic vents.

▲ *These deep blue crystals of boleite are named after Boleo in Baja, California.*

Anhydrite

- **This mineral is important** in the chemical industry. For many years it has been extracted for use in the production of sulphuric acid, fertilizers and insecticides.

- **Chemically, it is calcium sulphate**. Anhydrite is very similar to gypsum, but lacks gypsum's water molecules.

Anhydrite can change to gypsum in moist conditions.

It rarely forms crystals. Usually it is found as irregular masses or fibres.

It is a pale-coloured mineral, commonly grey, white or brownish. Some delicate blue and green specimens occur.

It can be told apart from gypsum by its greater hardness. Anhydrite can just be marked by a coin, whereas gypsum is easily scratched by a fingernail.

Anhydrite has an average density for minerals, and is 2.98 times denser than water.

This mineral usually occurs as an evaporite. It forms with a number of other minerals when lakes, and especially salt water lagoons, dry up, and salts that have been dissolved in the water crystallize.

- **Anhydrite is also found** where rocks containing gypsum have been altered, for example, by metamorphism.

- **Minerals occurring with anhydrite** include halite, calcite, gypsum and sylvine.

◀ *Pale blue is an unusual colour for anhydrite. This specimen shows a mass of flattened, prismatic crystals.*

Calcite and rhodochrosite

- **Calcite and rhodochrosite** are both carbonate minerals. They are made of a metal joined in a chemical compound with carbon and oxygen.

- **Calcite** (calcium carbonate) is one of the most common minerals. It is the main mineral in limestone, and metamorphic marbles are composed of calcite.

- **Hydrothermal veins** often contain calcite along with other minerals, such as galena, sphalerite and barite.

- **Calcite** is uncommon in igneous rocks. A group of volcanic and magmatic rocks called carbonatites are rich in carbonates. These are rare rocks usually found with syenite.

- **Calcite** defines point 3 on the hardness scale. It forms as sharply pointed or flattened six-sided crystals.

▲ *When calcite crystals have flattened tops they are called nail-head crystals.*

◀ *This type of rhodochrosite, with different coloured bands running through it, is often cut and polished ornamentally.*

● **Rhodochrosite** (manganese carbonate) is a rich, deep pinkish-red colour. Many minerals containing manganese are red.

● **Rhodochrosite** can form as crystals, but also occurs in rounded or nodular masses.

Both calcite and rhodochrosite dissolve in hydrochloric acid (the acid needs to be warm to react with rhodochrosite.) The bubbles given off are of carbon dioxide.

Rhodochrosite occurs in hydrothermal veins and where rocks rich in manganese have been altered.

Because of its attractive colour, rhodochrosite is cut and polished ornamentally.

Siderite and dolomite

- **These two minerals have** a number of similarities, but are easily told apart by other properties. Chemically they are both carbonates.

- **Siderite is a carbonate** of iron. It is a chemical compound of iron, carbon and oxygen. The carbon and oxygen together form the 'carbonate' part of the formula.

- **Dolomite is a carbonate of calcium** and magnesium. The word dolomite is also used as a rock name for the type of limestone that contains a high proportion of this mineral.

- **A similarity between these two minerals** is that their crystal faces are often curved.

- **Siderite is harder than a coin** but softer than a knife blade. Its hardness is 4. Its iron content gives it a density of about 4 times that of water.

- **This mineral is usually a dull colour** – grey, brown, black or red are typical.

- **Both these minerals** occur in mineral veins and in sedimentary rocks.

- **Softer than siderite**, dolomite's hardness is about the same as that of a coin, at $3\frac{1}{2}$ to 4. It has a density 2.85 times that of water, so is lighter than a same-sized specimen of siderite.

This mineral is often white, cream, pink or brown in colour.

Dolomite will dissolve in cold, weak hydrochloric acid. It does not produce the violent effervescence that calcite does.

▼ *In this specimen from a mineral vein in Durham, UK, siderite occurs as greyish crystals. The white and colourless transparent crystals are quartz.*

Strontianite and smithsonite

▲ *Although it can be a variety of colours, this sample of smithsonite from Tsumeb, Namibia, is grey in colour.*

● **Strontianite is named** after Strontian in Argyll, Scotland, where it has been mined.

The element strontium, which occurs in this mineral, is also named after Strontian. It was discovered in 1798 by Thomas Hope and first isolated in pure form in 1808 by British scientist, Sir Humphry Davy.

The mineral strontianite is a carbonate of strontium.

It occurs in mineral veins with other minerals, including the sulphides galena and sphalerite, and carbonates such as calcite and dolomite.

Strontianite is white, grey, yellow or green in colour, and has the same hardness as a coin (3½).

This mineral has a density of 3.7 times that of water.

Smithsonite is zinc carbonate also called Zincspar. It is an important ore of zinc.

It can be a very colourful mineral. Some specimens are a rich-blue colour. Others are white, pink, green or brown.

This mineral has a hardness of 4½ and a density of around 4.5.

...FASCINATING FACT...

Zinc has many important applications. It is used in batteries, and to galvanize (coat) steel to prevent rusting.

Witherite

- **This mineral is a carbonate** of the heavy metal barium.

- **Because of this chemical composition**, witherite has a relatively high density of 4.29.

- **Where it occurs** in large amounts, witherite is used as an ore of barium.

- **This metal has medical applications**. It is used for taking X-rays of the stomach and gut. It is also employed in the manufacture of specialized glass.

- **Witherite forms crystals** that have pyramids at both ends. It also occurs as fibrous, globular and irregular forms.

- **When light falls on the crystal faces**, they shine like glass, and light may pass through the crystal.

- **It can be a variety** of colours. It is sometimes green, but is more often white, brown or grey.

- **This mineral** has the same hardness as a coin, at 3½.

- **Along with minerals** including quartz, calcite, barite and galena, witherite occurs in mineral veins.

- **Witherite reacts strongly** with dilute, cold hydrochloric acid. It can be distinguished from calcite, which also does this, by its greater density.

▼ *These greyish, flattened crystals of witherite are from Brancepeth in Durham, UK.*

Cerussite and aurichalcite

- **The main carbonate** of lead is cerussite, while aurichalcite is a hydrous carbonate of zinc and copper.

- **Cerussite contains lead**, which makes it a very dense mineral – 6.55 times more dense than water.

- **One of the most striking features** of cerussite is its crystal form. It frequently occurs as masses of thin, elongated crystals.

- **Usually cerussite is pale coloured**, cream, grey, white and yellow, although it can be green or blue.

- **Cerussite is easily scratched** by a steel knife blade, and may just be marked by a coin. Its hardness is 3 to 3½.

- **This mineral forms** in mineral veins containing lead, copper and zinc, which have been altered by water and other fluids seeping through them.

- **Aurichalcite is a striking green** or blue mineral, which is prized by mineral collectors.

- **Although other properties** are also important, it is easily recognized by both its colour and softness. It can be scratched with a fingernail.

- **It forms in altered mineral veins**, and frequently occurs as coatings of small crystals, or rounded masses, on rock surfaces.

- **Like a number of minerals**, aurichalcite effervesces (bubbles up) in cold, dilute hydrochloric acid. Its colour and hardness distinguish it from calcite and witherite.

◄ *Cerussite often occurs in thin masses of prismatic crystals, which look like straw.*

Ulexite

- **Classified as a borate**, ulexite contains sodium, calcium, boron and oxygen joined in a chemical compound to molecules of water.

- **This mineral has been used** as an ore of boron. Compounds of this element are used to toughen glass, and in microchips and paper-making.

- **It often occurs as rounded masses**, but long, fibrous aggregates or fluffy-looking lumps called 'cotton balls' made of many thin crystals are also found

▼ *When lakes dry out in arid regions, a variety of minerals can form as the water evaporates. Ulexite is an evaporite mineral formed in this situation.*

▼ *Ulexite often occurs with borax in evaporite deposits. Together the two minerals are a source of boron.*

Ulexite is very soft. It can be marked easily with a coin and sometimes by a fingernail.

This mineral has very low density – only twice the density of water.

Masses of ulexite are pale in colour, usually white or colourless, with a silky sheen on the surface.

Many crystals of ulexite are transparent, allowing light to pass through them.

A special property of this mineral is that it can dissolve in hot water.

Ulexite forms during the evaporation and drying out of lakes in desert regions, such as the Californian Desert.

...FASCINATING FACT...
Crystal masses of ulexite have fibre optical properties. If these masses are polished at their ends, light and images can be transmitted along the crystals, giving it the alternative name 'television stone'.

Strange mineral properties

- **Because of their chemistry** or crystal structure, a number of minerals have properties that are special to them, and by which they can be readily identified.

- **A transparent crystal** of calcite is called Iceland spar. When an object is seen through such a crystal, it appears double. This is called double refraction.

- **Many minerals** react with acids. It is best only to test them with weak hydrochloric acid. Certain sulphides, such as galena, release hydrogen sulphide gas when reacting with this acid.

- **Certain minerals** that contain iron are magnetic. Magnetite attracts iron filings. Hematite becomes magnetic when it is heated.

- **Ruby, sapphire** and some other minerals contain minute criss-cross needles of rutile that produce a shining starshape when light shines on them. This optical property is known as asterism.

- **Quartz**, tourmaline and hemimorphite all develop electrical potential when subjected to mechanical stress.

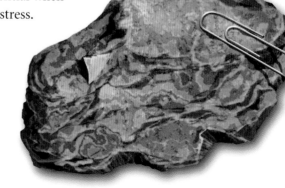

▶ *Magnetite, as its name suggests, is magnetic. This specimen has attracted a paper clip.*

► *Iceland spar is remarkable because it shows double refraction – objects seen through a crystal appear double.*

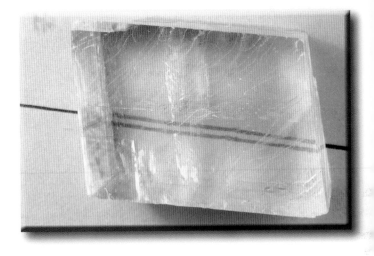

Talc and molybdenite are flexible and can be bent. Mica, if bent, is flexible and reverts to its original shape.

When a mineral has a high-temperature flame directed onto it, the colours produced are related to the mineral's chemistry. Sodium minerals colour the flame yellow, potassium gives a violet flame, and copper colours the flame green.

Halite, nitrate minerals and some sulphates are soluble in water. Specimens of these have to be carefully stored.

... **FASCINATING FACT** ...
Chatoyancy produces a thin band of light through a mineral, like the structure of a cat's eye. Chrysoberyl, quartz and moonstone can show this property.

Barite and celestite

▶ *A group of delicate blue celestite crystals. This mineral is an ore of strontium.*

- **Barite and celestite** are both sulphates. Barite contains the metal barium and celestite contains strontium.

- **They can both occur in** hydrothermal veins with a range of minerals, including quartz, galena, sphalerite, calcite and dolomite.

- **Barite** may occur around hot springs and in nodules in clay. Celestite can be found in evaporite deposits and hydrothermal veins.

◀ *Some of these barite crystals have been coloured by iron-rich fluids. Barite is one of the densest minerals found in mineral veins.*

Barite is usually pale-coloured and can be white, colourless and transparent, pink, brown or grey. Fine crystals of barite are common and it also forms rounded masses called cockscomb barite.

Because it contains barium, barite is a dense mineral. It weighs 4.5 times as much as an equal volume of water. This property helps to tell barite from other common pale-coloured vein minerals.

Barite is the main ore of barium metal. It is used in 'drilling mud', a lubricant employed when drilling for oil.

Celestite can be colourless, grey, white, blue or green and often forms shiny crystals, like those of barite.

Celestite fluoresces under ultra-violet light, and is slightly soluble in water.

Strontium is used in the manufacture of paint, car batteries, fireworks, glass and flares.

▶ *The element strontium, which occurs in celestite, is used in fireworks. Strontium gives burning fireworks a rich red colour.*

Kyanite and garnet

- **Many minerals** develop during metamorphism. Two of the most attractive are kyanite and garnet.

- **Kyanite** forms in rocks that have been regionally metamorphosed under conditions of considerable pressure and temperature.

- **Schist and gneiss** are the rocks in which kyanite usually occurs.

- **Kyanite** is often various shades of blue but may also be pink, green, grey or yellow.

- **In schist and gneiss**, kyanite occurs as long, thin, bladed crystals.

- **An interesting feature** of kyanite is its varying hardness. This ranges between 4 and 7, depending on the direction in which it is scratched.

▶ *This fine mass of blue, blade-shaped kyanite crystals is from Brazil.*

264

Garnet is really the name for a family of minerals. Each garnet has slightly different chemical properties.

Garnet commonly forms as crystals in the cubic system. The crystals are rarely simple cubes, but more usually complex shapes with parallelogram faces.

Garnets can be dark red-brown, green, orange or red.

Because it is harder than quartz and has attractive colours, garnet is used as a gemstone.

◀ *There are many different named types of garnet. This red-brown variety is called grossular.*

Malachite and azurite

- **Malachite and azurite** have been prized since the Bronze Age for their colours. The two minerals often occur together in mineral veins.

- **Both malachite and azurite** are copper-bearing minerals. They are copper carbonates.

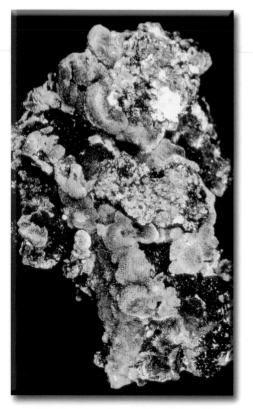

- **Where copper veins** have been altered by weathering and contact with fluids, malachite and azurite may be found.

- **A useful test** for both minerals is applying dilute, cold hydrochloric acid to them. A chemical reaction will occur, producing bubbles of carbon dioxide.

- **Malachite** is a brilliant deep green colour, and has been used as a paint pigment for over 3000 years.

◀ *This specimen of malachite shows the rounded botryoidal habit. Though it is very soft, malachite is cut and polished for jewellery.*

▲ *Small crystals of deep blue azurite coat this rock surface. This specimen is from the Atlas Mountains, Morocco.*

As it is a soft mineral (hardness 4), malachite can be easily shaped and polished ornamentally.

Malachite often forms in rounded, botryoidal masses. When cut and polished, curved patterns can appear.

Azurite is a rich, deep blue colour. This mineral has also been exploited as paint pigment for thousands of years.

Azurite occurs in rounded masses and also as short, stocky crystals.

With a hardness of only 4, azurite can be easily scratched with a knife.

Fluorite

- **Fluorite** is a common mineral in hydrothermal veins, where it occurs with galena, calcite, quartz, borite and sphalerite.

- **Because of its chemical composition**, fluorite (calcium fluoride) has some important uses. It is used in the manufacture of hydrofluoric acid and the fluorine chemicals.

- **Fluorite forms cubic** and octahedral crystals. Perfect lenses can be manufactured from fluorite crystals.

▼ *These pale green, cubic crystals of fluorite are transparent allowing light to pass through them.*

▶ *As well as forming fine crystals, fluorite also occurs in bands of different colours. This polished specimen from China has a thin layer of pyrite on its surface.*

In the iron and steel industry, fluorite is used as a flux. This is a material added to the molten metal to take out impurities and form the slag.

In the past, fluorite was often discarded when mineral veins were mined for lead and zinc. For this reason fine specimens can be found on old mine dumps.

Fluorite is the defining mineral at point 4 on the hardness scale.

An attractive banded form of fluorite, which is found in Derbyshire, UK, is called Blue John. This is cut and polished ornamentally.

Fluorite is commonly purple, green or yellowish and the crystals are transparent.

Often fluorite crystals interlock. This property is called twinning. When seen in ultra-violet light, fluorite is strongly fluorescent.

...FASCINATING FACT...
Fluorite is sometimes cut and facetted
as an imitation diamond.

Zeolite minerals

▼ *This specimen shows fine crystals of the zeolite mineral, stilbite, growing into a cavity in basalt lava. The crystals are 1 cm long.*

Zeolites usually occur in the gas bubble hollows, called vesicles, in lavas. These hollows are left as the lava cools and gas escapes.

They are a group of silicate minerals that have molecules of water in their chemical structure.

These minerals form when hot water and other fluids seep through lava that has been cool for some time and buried in the Earth's crust.

Amygdales are the infilled gas bubble cavities in lava. Amygdales can be made of quartz and agate as well as zeolite.

They have an open crystal structure, rather like a miniature sieve. For this reason, zeolites are used to soak up moisture in industrial processes.

Most zeolites are pale-coloured. They usually form good crystals, often in a mass of thin radiating shapes.

Zeolites often occur in concentric zones in thick lava flows.

Stilbite is an unusual zeolite, as the crystals are in sheaflike aggregates.

Zeolites are also used as water softeners, as they are able to exchange ions. The sodium-rich zeolite called natrolite will take calcium out of hard water by exchanging its sodium for calcium.

... FASCINATING FACT ...
The 'silica gel' found in small packets with cameras and electrical equipment has a zeolite structure.

Jet

- **Jet is an organic material** that is often classified with minerals.

- **The term 'jet black'** comes from this material, which is often found as layers or discrete masses in sedimentary rocks. It is therefore regarded as a sedimentary rock by many geologists.

- **Much jet** comes from the Lower Jurassic strata.

- **Jet is a type** of coal. It has a high carbon content and is formed from plant material, especially the tree *Araucaria*, commonly known as the monkey puzzle tree.

- **Unlike other types** of coal, jet is found in strata deposited in the sea. Logs and other plant remains probably drifted out into the Jurassic sea, and when waterlogged they sank, to be buried under sediment.

▲ *The modern monkey puzzle tree is a close relative of the plants from which jet formed.*

- **The heat and pressure** from overlying layers of sediment converted the plant material into jet.

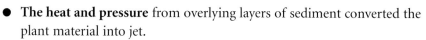

Because jet is relatively soft, it can be easily carved. It can also be very highly polished and so is used in jewellery.

Jet has been cut and polished since the Bronze Age. The ancient Romans in particular prized jewellery made from jet.

Queen Victoria popularized jet jewellery in the 19th century after the death of her husband, Prince Albert. Jet was extensively mined at that time.

Jet has become popular again in recent years. There are many fake items that are passed off as jet. These are usually made of man-made materials, including plastics.

▶ *An ancient Roman jet bangle. Jet has been cut and worked for jewellery and ornaments for over 2000 years.*

Amber

- **Amber** is the fossilized resin from ancient conifer trees, and can occur in sedimentary rocks of Cenozoic Age.

- **Amber** is an organic mineral that occurs as nodules and discrete lumps.

- **As well as** the typical pale orange, it can also be brown, greenish and black.

- **Amber is very soft** and has a splintery fracture. The surface appears resinous and transparent.

- **Much amber** is found as small 'pebbles' on beaches.

- **It is only just denser** than water and can be carried by the sea. Large amounts of amber occur in the Baltic area.

- **Amber** also occurs in Romania, Italy, France, Spain, Canada, the Dominican Republic and Russia.

- **Amber often contains** small bubbles. This is called nebulous amber.

◀ *This fossil fly has remained unaltered since it was trapped in resin oozing from a pine tree. The resin is now amber.*

Amber is very easy to carve and for many years has been used for jewellery.

Fossils are often found in amber. These are usually fossils of small insects that were stuck in fragrant resin oozing from a tree. This hardened to become amber.

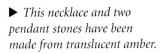

▶ *This necklace and two pendant stones have been made from translucent amber.*

Sapphire and ruby

- **Corundum** is aluminium oxide and is the second-hardest mineral to diamond.

- **Usually**, corundum forms as six-sided (hexagonal) crystals with pyramids a the top and bottom.

- **Corundum** can occur in many colours, including pink, yellow, grey, green and brown. Bright red corundum is ruby and blue corundum is sapphire.

- **Because of its great hardness** and rich colours, corundum is much valued a a gemstone.

- **Corundum** forms in igneous and metamorphic rocks, but most of the gem quality stones are found in river shingle. This is an example of a placer deposit, where hard resistant minerals have been re-deposited after erosion and transport.

- **Famous sources** of gem corundum are Sri Lanka, Kashmir, Australia, Thailand and eastern Africa.

- **Certain rubies** are called star rubies. These show asterism, as small needles of rutile make a star effect in the ruby.

- **Corundum** is used as an abrasive. Emery is an impure form of corundum that often also contains iron minerals.

- **Corundum can be made** artificially. August Verneuil perfected the techniqu as long ago as 1900.

...FASCINATING FACT...
Corundum crystals weighing 170 kg have
been found in South Africa.

▲ *These ruby crystals from India are in a specimen of metamorphic rock called gneiss. The pale crystals are quartz.*

Decorative non-crystalline minerals

- **Many minerals** that are non-crystalline have great value as ornamental stones, usually because of their colours.

- **The deep blue** lapis lazuli is mainly composed of lazurite. The finest material comes from Afghanistan. Russia and China are other sources.

- **Lazurite** contains veins of white calcite and pyrite. It is about as hard as a knife blade (hardness 5), and is translucent. Lapis is much used for jewellery.

- **Turquoise** is another blue, decorative mineral, though it is generally paler than lapis lazuli.

- **Turquoise can be green** if it contains much iron. Its blue colour comes from a high copper content.

- **Much of the attractiveness** of turquoise lies in the veins of darker material that often run through it.

- **Jade** is the name given to the ornamental form of the minerals jadeite and nephrite.

- **Jadeite and nephrite** are as hard as quartz. The green variety of each is the most prized for carving.

- **Rhodonite**, a complex silicate mineral, has an attractive pink colour due to the manganese in its structure.

Rhodonite is used for carving and its hardness grading of 6 makes it reasonably resistant to wear.

Green 'jade' can be either nephrite or jadeite. These polished examples, and the slab they re on, are made of the mineral nephrite.

279

Minerals at home

▶ *If you look at grains of salt with a magnifying glass, the small cubic crystals of halite are clearly visible.*

- **A wide range of minerals** and their constituents are used in the home. These range from structural and mechanical components to food.

- **Cement**, which holds the brick or stone of walls together, is made of calcite (calcium carbonate) and mudstone. Cement is mixed with sand, which is mainly quartz.

- **Internal walls** are made smooth with plaster, which is composed largely of gypsum (calcium sulphate).

- **Electricity** is carried through the house in copper wires and water flows through copper pipes.

- **Steel**, made from iron ore (hematite and magnetite), is used for supporting lintels. It is also used to make cutlery, furniture and many other items around the home.

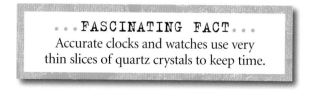

. . . **FASCINATING FACT** . . .
Accurate clocks and watches use very
thin slices of quartz crystals to keep time.

Within the home, aluminium (from bauxite) is a common metal. It is used in cooking containers, cooking foil and washing machines.

Glass is manufactured from quartz sand. It is melted and shaped into sheets or utensils. Around 2000 years ago the Romans were one of the first civilizations to make glass from quartz.

Salt in the kitchen and on the dinner table is halite (sodium chloride).

Cars contain aluminium (bauxite), steel (iron ores) and copper. A car battery uses lead plates (galena) to produce an electric current.

▶ *Many domestic appliances, such as washing machines, contain metals extracted from minerals. Aluminium (from bauxite), steel (iron from hematite and magnetite) and copper (native copper or chalcopyrite).*

What are fossils?

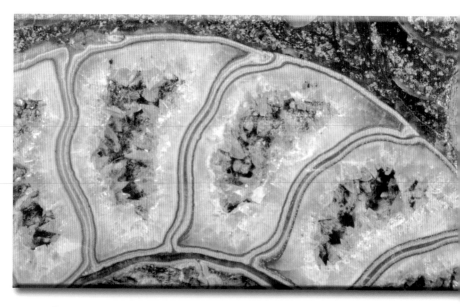

▲ *The internal chambers of this ammonite shell have filled with crystals of calcite during fossilization.*

- **Fossils** are the remains of, or evidence for, past life preserved in the rocks of the Earth's crust.

- **For the remains** of an organism to be preserved, it has to be made of material that is stable in the sediment (mud and sand) in which it is buried.

- **Usually shells**, bones, plant stems and other remains are changed into minerals, such as calcite and quartz, for them to be preserved.

- **Creatures and plants** with hard parts are more easily preserved, as they are not easily broken before they are buried in sediment.

Some fossils are simply the impressions of a shell or other organism on a rock surface. All the solid parts of the creature have disappeared.

Most fossils are of organisms that lived in the sea, because here most sediment is deposited.

Sometimes, whole organisms are preserved almost unaltered, such as insects trapped in amber, or mammals preserved in frozen ground.

Only the tiniest fraction of creatures and plants that have lived are preserved in the 'fossil record'.

Scientists who study fossils are called palaeontologists and the science is called palaeontology.

...FASCINATING FACT...
Some of the most delicate organic remains that have been fossilized include the feathers of primitive birds, the wings of dragonflies and the leaves of plants.

Fossils and time

- **Palaeontologists** are able to use fossils to work out many details about the Earth in the past, including how old strata (rock layers) are.

- **The sediments** in which fossils are preserved were deposited in layers, with the older layers below younger ones.

- **Certain strata** are characterized by particular fossils, and these rocks can be correlated from place to place by using their fossils.

- **Fossils** that are widespread geographically are best for this linking of strata from one area to another.

- **Fossils from the Jurassic Period** found in Britain, Europe, the Himalayas and South America tell us that rocks in these now distant regions formed at exactly the same time.

- **Fossilized species** that only existed for a short time will only be found in a relatively thin layer of rock, and so will allow accurate correlation.

- **Ammonites and graptolites** are excellent for the relative dating of rocks.

◀ *This large ammonite, fossilized in limestone, has been eroded to reveal the suture lines*

The relative geological time scale has been established by using fossils and other geological principles.

Radiometric dating is used to give absolute dates to the various parts of the time scale.

The time represented by a given fossil species is called a zone, and may be as brief as 750,000 years.

▼ *This time chart shows how geological time has been divided by geologists. The absolute dates (the numbers) have been worked out using radiometric dating methods.*

ERA	PERIOD	EPOCH	AGE (MYA)
CENOZOIC	Neogene	Holocene (Recent)	From 0.01
			1.8–0.01
		Pleistocene	5.3–1.8
		Pliocene	23–5.3
		Miocene	
	Palaeogene	Oligocene	34–23
		Eocene	56–34
		Palaeocene	65–56
MESOZOIC	Cretaceous		142–65
	Jurassic		206–142
	Triassic		248–206
PALAEOZOIC	Permian		290–248
	Carboniferous		354–290
	Devonian		417–354
	Silurian		443–417
	Ordovician		495–443
	Cambrian		545–495
PRE-CAMBRIAN TIME			4500–545

Collecting fossil

- **Some of the most famous** and important fossils have been found by chanc but it is wise to make plans before you go collecting.

- **Fossils occur** mainly in sedimentary rocks, so there is no point looking in areas where granite or other igneous rocks occur.

- **Sedimentary rocks** such as limestone, mudstone, sandstone and shale are formed in layers, usually on the seabed.

- **Road cuttings**, stream valleys and sea shores are good places to look for fossils, as here strata are exposed and can be easily seen.

- **A geological map** is useful to find out where sedimentary rocks, which may contain fossils, occur, but a map may not show exactly where the rocks are exposed. Strata are often obscured by buildings and roads, soil, plants and trees, and glacial debris.

- **Rocky coasts** are very good places to find fossils, as here rocks are constantl being eroded. Cliff falls bring fossil-bearing rock down to beach level. However, they should be approached with caution. Many geologists have been injured, and some killed, by rock falls from cliffs.

- **Permission** must always be sought before going onto private land, and you should never go alone.

- **A geological hammer** is useful for breaking up rocks containing fossils. Do not use an ordinary woodwork hammer, as the metal it is made of is very soft.

- **There is often no need** to quarry away at strata. Fossils are readily obtained from fallen and eroded rocks.

- **All fossils** are of scientific importance. Always wrap any specimens carefull and record in a notebook where and when you found them.

▲ *Fossils have to be carefully removed. Here, dinosaur bones are encased in plaster before they are carried away.*

287

Naming and caring for fossils

- **Fossils are biological material**, and they are named according to the principles of biology.

- **This system**, still used today, was established in the 18th century by Carolus Linnaeus, a Swedish naturalist. Because there was a different name for each plant and animal in each language, he used mainly Latin names.

- **An organism** is generally given two names. The first is its generic name and the second its specific name.

- **The ammonite** *Hildoceras bifrons* belongs to the genus *Hildoceras*. This contains a number of species, of which *bifrons* is one. Note that biological names are written in italics.

- **These Latin words** have significance and meaning. *Hildoceras*, for example, is named after St Hilda, whose Abbey is at Whitby in North Yorkshire. This ammonite is common in strata there. The species name *'bifrons'* describes the two 'brows' or ridges running around the edge of the fossil.

- **To name fossils** that you have found, it will usually be necessary to compare them with those shown in one of the many illustrated palaeontology books or Internet sites.

- **Expert help** will be available at a local museum or university if you are unable to work out the name for a certain fossil.

- **Your fossils** will have to be cleaned, and any excess rock or dirt carefully removed.

◀ *These fossil molluscs have been placed in card trays, with labels to stop them rubbing against one another.*

- **It is best** to keep each fossil in a small card tray, so that there is no chance of them rubbing together.

- **The details of each fossil**, taken from your notebook, can be written on a card beneath the specimen. A number of these trays can be kept in a single drawer.

289

Extinction

- **When a species dies out**, for whatever reason, it is said to be extinct. Simil? species may continue to survive, but that unique species has gone forever.

- **The fossil record** contains many breaks. A series of fossils that can be trace from layer to layer may suddenly come to an end, showing that those creatures became extinct.

- **Extinction** of one group of organisms can allow another to develop and flourish, so extinction allows the evolution of other species to take place.

- **There are countless** examples of extinction to be found when fossils are studied, from the dinosaurs to small molluscs.

- **The causes of extinction** are varied, but environmental changes can cause the death of many unrelated species, as may have happened at the end of the Permian Period, 248 million years ago.

- **A classic case** of extinction, which has been studied in detail, is that of the dinosaurs at the end of the Cretaceous Period, 65 million years ago.

- **There is considerable evidence** for a widespread change in climate and sea levels at the end of the Cretaceous Period.

- **Evidence** from various places shows that a large meteorite may have hit the Earth at about this time.

Dust from this meteorite impact would obscure the sunlight and kill plants. Food chains would then be destroyed, causing widespread extinction of many different animals.

> ...FASCINATING FACT...
> When the dinosaurs became extinct, so did 75 percent of marine plankton, and very successful creatures such as the marine ammonites.

Ammonite fossils. Ammonites became extinct at the end of the Cretaceous Period, 65 million years ago.

Evolution

● **Evidence** for the development of life into its various forms can be found in the record of fossils. This change from one living thing to another is called evolution.

● **By looking at fossils**, it can clearly be seen that the more primitive plants and animals are found in the oldest rocks. However, the trilobites, which occured as long ago as the Cambrian Period (545–495 million years ago), were very well-developed creatures.

● **Evolution** is not always a steady process. It has many sudden jumps when organisms develop rapidly.

▼ *Trilobites appeared at the beginning of the Cambrian Period. They probably evolved from soft-bodied pre-Cambrian creatures.*

● **During the Pre-Cambrian Era** (before 545 million years ago) life was probably very primitive, but for various reasons the fossil record from this time is extremely sparse.

● **At the start** of the Cambrian Period a rapid explosion of life forms occured. Trilobites and many other invertebrates were suddenly numerous.

● **In the Jurassic Period** (206–142 million years ago) sea urchins suddenly developed and evolved.

◄ *Charles Darwin was one of the first scientists to publish a theory of evolution of organisms.*

Charles Darwin's famous book on evolution *The Origin of the Species*, was published in 1859. His theories of natural selection and the survival of the organisms best suited to a certain habitat are still accepted by most scientists today.

Modern scientists are trying to increase our knowledge of evolution. Darwin didn't have access to new scientific ideas about DNA and genetics.

Mutation is one of the keys to evolution. It is a change in the DNA of an organism, which may occur because of chemical or environmental influence.

Humans have influenced the evolution of various organisms. Where industrial pollution has produced dark, grimy tree trunks, a dark form of the peppered moth has evolved, which is camouflaged in this habitat. Human misuse of the environment has driven many species to extinction.

Tracks, trails and burrows

- **Sedimentary rocks** can be formed as layers on the seabed, the land surface, a lake or river bed. These layers (strata) were at one time the Earth's surface, and they often have puzzling grooves and trails running over them.

- **Along with a wide range** of other structures, these trails are called trace fossils.

- **A fossil**, the record of past life, does not have to be a shell, bone or leaf. It can be a burrow, track, eggshell or dropping that tells us that a creature or plant has existed.

- **The study of** these trace fossils is called ichnology.

- **Trace fossils** are given scientific names, like other fossils.

- **Some of the most famous** trace fossils are dinosaur footprints. These can be used to work out the size and speed of a dinosaur.

▲ *These narrow grooves were probably made by molluscs moving over wet mud on the Carboniferous seabed.*

294

For a trace fossil, such as a burrow or arthropod track, to be preserved, it must be filled in with mud or sand very soon after it is made, or it will be washed away.

In some cases, the fossil of the mollusc or shrimp that has made a trace fossil is found at the end of its fossil burrow.

Dinosaur eggs are trace fossils. Nests of *Protoceratops'* eggs and young have been found in Mongolia.

A trace fossil called *Cruziana* occurs in many strata of Palaeozoic and Mesozoic age. Originally, it was thought to be the trail of a trilobite, but these arthropods became extinct in the late Palaeozoic. It is possible that a number of different arthropods made very similar trails.

▶ *Dinosaurs, like this* Protoceratops, *scraped nests in the ground in which to lay their eggs.*

Rocks made of fossils

- **Some sedimentary rocks** are made almost entirely of fossils and fossil fragments.

- **Coal**, which has been one of the most important fuels since the 1800s, is made of the altered fossil remains of plants.

- **The finest fossils** are usually found in rocks that are made of very small particles of sediment. These are able to preserve details. Also, such sediment is less likely to crush the original organism as it is buried.

- **There are a number** of types of limestone that are classified as organic limestone, meaning that they are largely made of fossil remains.

- **Crinoids** are marine organisms related to starfish and sea urchins. They are made of calcite, and have a long, brittle stem that raises the animal off the seabed. Their broken remains, stuck together with lime mud, make crinoidal limestone – common in the Carboniferous system.

- **Chalk** is a very fine-grained, almost dusty, limestone, mainly formed during the Cretaceous Period, 142–65 million years ago. It is made of countless minute fossils, including coccoliths.

- **Coral reefs**, not unlike those that occur today, have existed at many times during the past. These reefs, rich in brachiopods, trilobites, molluscs and corals, are sometimes preserved as fossil-rich limestone.

- **Shelly limestone** is a term used by geologists for a rock composed mainly of fossil shells. These may be of molluscs or brachiopods (lampshells).

● **Shelly limestones** may once have been banks of shells washed together by sea currents.

● **Even when** there seems to be no fossils in a rock, it may still be made largely of fossil fragments. The use of a x10 hand lens will show this.

◄ *The chalk in this cliff is almost entirely composed of fossil material, mainly tiny sea organisms called coccoliths.*

297

Microfossils

- **Microfossils** are tiny fossils that can only be studied with the help of a microscope. There is no actual agreed size below which a fossil is considered a microfossil. When seen at high magnification, microfossils reveal a remarkable array of shapes and structures.

- **The larger fossils**, such as shells, bones, teeth and plant remains, are called macrofossils.

- **Microfossils are widespread** and commonly overlooked. Most sedimentary rocks contain microfossils, and a study of these can give important details about the age and environment in which the rock was formed.

- **Many microfossils** are of single-celled organisms, and the use of an electron microscope is necessary to study them.

- **The study** of fossil pollen, palynology, is a branch of micropalaeontology. Pollen is a very good indicator of past climates.

- **The pure-white** limestone called chalk is made up of microfossils including coccoliths. These are single-celled, planktonic organisms with a circular structure. They are most numerous in warm seawater.

- **At certain points** in the geological record there are rocks referred to as cherts. These are silica-rich sediments, some of which are formed by accumulations of microfossils called *Radiolaria*.

- **Conodonts** are minute, toothlike fossils. Exactly what they are has been a matter of discussion. Studies of complete conodont fossils suggest that it may have been an eellike creature. They only occur in rocks from the Cambrian to Triassic ages.

▲ *Among the commonest fossils are minute microfossils. These diatoms (minute, single-celled algae) are magnified many hundreds of times.*

Foraminifera are single-celled organisms that live as plankton or on the seabed. Their tiny shells make up much of the 'ooze' that covers the deep ocean floor.

Nummulites are slightly larger types of Foraminifera that often make up nummulitic limestone. This rock was used a lot as a building stone in ancient Egypt.

299

The oldest fossil:

- **The record of fossils** from Pre-Cambrian times (4600–545 million years ago) is remarkably sparse. This is most of geological time, and yet we know very little about what was alive then.

- **Pre-Cambrian rocks** are often changed by metamorphism, and so any fossils they may have contained could have been removed.

- **Primitive life forms** would have had soft bodies, probably without shells, so may not have been preserved as fossils.

- **In its early years**, the Earth's atmosphere lacked oxygen and may have been composed of gases such as water vapour, methane and ammonia. These are not useful to life as we know it today.

◀ *During the end of the Pre-Cambrian Period many organisms developed, including these fronds of* Charnia, *probably a sea pen.*

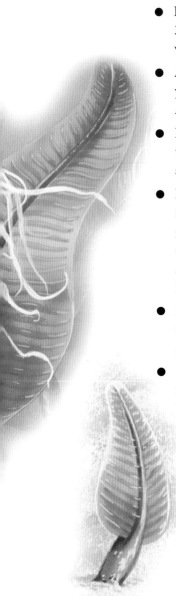

- **Life probably** first developed around 3500 million years ago, though there is very little fossil evidence from this time.

- **Among the earliest** fossils are 3500 million-year-old algal remains found in Western Australia.

- **In the silica-rich** chert near Lake Superior in the US, fossil microscopic plant cells occur, suggesting that there was more oxygen about.

- **Late in the Pre-Cambrian**, organisms became more numerous. One of the most famous groups of fossils, the 'Ediacaran assemblage', comes from a number of sites, including Australia, England, Newfoundland, Scandinavia, Russia and Africa.

- **Ediacaran fossils** include delicate organisms such as jellyfish, worms, frondlike organisms and sea pens.

- *Charnia* is a famous Ediacaran fossil found in 1957 in Charnwood Forest, Leicestershire, by a schoolboy.

301

Fossil algae

- **Though they are very delicate organisms**, certain algae build calcium carbonate structures that are easily preserved as fossils.

- **The best-known fossil** algal structures are called stromatolites, made by blue-green algae.

- **Algae and bacteria** work together to build the rounded mounds of layered calcium carbonate.

- **When seen in a rock face**, stromatolites are mounds of calcite. On a flat surface they look like concentrically banded discs.

- **The earliest stromatolites** are found in rocks over 3000 million years old.

- **In the 1950s**, living stromatolite-building algae were found in Western Australia. Here they exist in water that is highly saline, where other organisms can't survive.

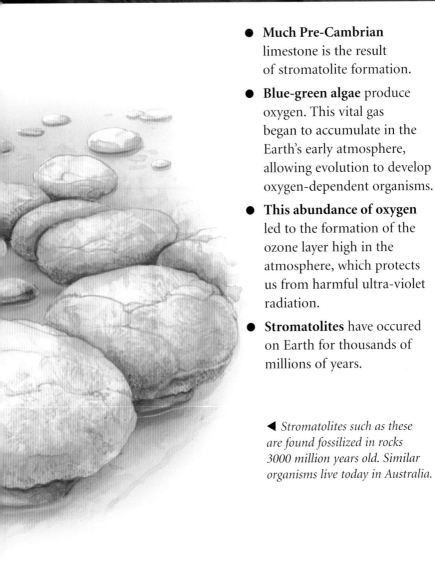

- **Much Pre-Cambrian** limestone is the result of stromatolite formation.

- **Blue-green algae** produce oxygen. This vital gas began to accumulate in the Earth's early atmosphere, allowing evolution to develop oxygen-dependent organisms.

- **This abundance of oxygen** led to the formation of the ozone layer high in the atmosphere, which protects us from harmful ultra-violet radiation.

- **Stromatolites** have occured on Earth for thousands of millions of years.

◄ *Stromatolites such as these are found fossilized in rocks 3000 million years old. Similar organisms live today in Australia.*

303

Primitive plants

- **The first vascular plants** (plants with veins) evolved in the late Palaeozoic Era.

- **In Devonian rocks** there is evidence of a rapid evolution of plants, and the Earth's surface began to look green for the first time.

- *Cooksonia* is a very early veined plant and occurred in rocks of late Silurian and Devonian age. During this period there were large landmasses on which vegetation could develop.

- **With a stiff stem**, *Cooksonia* could stand up above the surface, in which it was held by primitive roots.

- **Like modern plants**, *Cooksonia* had xylem cells that were able to transport water through the plant.

- **The fossil plant *Parka*** is also from the Devonian Period. Both *Cooksonia* and *Parka* probably reproduced with spores.

◀ *This reconstruction of* Cooksonia *shows its delicate branching stems and fruiting masses.*

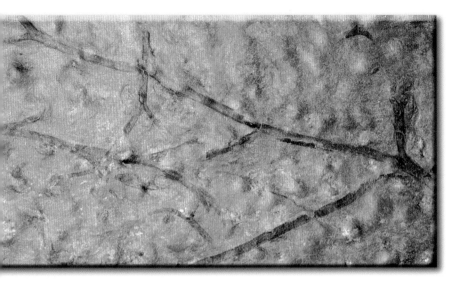

▲ *These slender stems of* Cooksonia, *one of the first land plants, were found in rocks of Devonian age in Orkney, Scotland.*

Like many fossil plants, these early Devonian species are preserved as thin carbon films, the rest of the plant tissue being lost during fossilization.

One of the best examples of early plant preservation is a rock formation called the Rhynie chert, found in Devonian rocks in Scotland. Here, early plants are preserved three-dimensionally in silica.

Microscope analysis of these silica fossils shows all their soft parts, allowing cellular structures to be examined.

It is probable that the Rhynie chert was deposited by hot springs, the plant remains washing in from nearby.

Fossil plants and coal

- **When plants grow**, their energy is largely obtained from sunlight, which they use for photosynthesis and tissue development. This energy is locked away, but is released when coal formed from plants is burnt.

- **Coal is formed** when plant material is buried, compressed and heated.

- **The most important** deposits of coal, formed in the Carboniferous Period, occur in the UK, North America, Belgium, France, Australia and Siberia.

- **Coal of Permian**, Triassic and Jurassic age is important in China, Europe and the USA. Coal from the Jurassic Period can be found in parts of the UK especially northeast Scotland.

- **As coal is formed** from advanced land plants, no coal of any value built up before Carboniferous times, when vast forests grew in the swamps.

Carboniferous coal-forming forests grew in warm, sub-tropical areas where rainfall was high, allowing rapid growth of giant horsetails and clubmosses.

The development of brown, damp peat is the first stage in coal formation.

Peat is used as a fuel in many parts of the world, but it doesn't burn at such a high temperature as coal.

In Ireland, and many other countries including Russia, there are power stations that generate electricity by burning peat.

As peat is buried under thousands of metres of sediment, it is heated and all impurities are removed. This increases the percentage of carbon, and turns the peat into coal.

▼ *Swamp forests, which produced coal, developed at many times in the past. This reconstruction shows a forest of Jurassic age.*

Coal-forming plants

- **The richest deposits of coal** have been formed by the accumulation of peat from forests. Coal-forming forests flourished in the Carboniferous Period.

- **As these forests grew** on the swampy top of vast deltas, they were flooded by the sea numerous times. This flooding brought sand and silt onto the delta in which fossil plants are often preserved.

- **A great variety of plants** grew in Carboniferous forests, including giant horsetails, clubmosses and seed ferns.

- *Lepidodendron* is a common fossil clubmoss from Carboniferous strata. It grew to over 30 m in height. The roots of this clubmoss are usually found as separate fossils, and are called *Stigmaria*.

- *Lepidodendron* **stems** can be recognized by their diamond-shaped leaf scars.

- **Another common** Carboniferous coal fossil is the giant horsetail, *Calamites*. Today, horsetails are relatively small plants that live in damp ground. *Calamites* grew to around 30 m tall.

- **Horsetails** have soft tissue inside their stems, which decays rapidly when they die. During fossilization, the stems often filled with sediment, so they are preserved in three dimensions.

- **A group of smaller plants** that helped make coal were called seed ferns.

- **Seed ferns** are plants with fernlike leaves, often preserved as carbon films on bedding planes.

- **Common Carboniferous** seed ferns include *Neuropteris*, *Eupecopteris* and *Sphenopteris*.

▼ *These alternating coal, shale and sandstone strata are on the coast of Fife, Scotland. The darker layers are coal made from plants that grew in the Carboniferous delta forests.*

Mazon Creek, Illinois

- **At certain times** in the fossil record a number of remarkably detailed accumulations of fossils occured.

- **At Mazon Creek in Illinois**, coal has been strip-mined for many tens of years. Above the coal layers there are mudstones, in which rounded, iron-rich lumps, called nodules, occur.

- **Nodules like these** are common in mudstone and shale of different ages. Their importance is that fossils contained in them are often beautifully preserved in great detail.

- **It is thought** that these, and nodules in other strata, often form chemically around organic remains.

- **Plant fossils**, especially leaves, are commonly crushed on bedding planes, but in the Mazon Creek nodules, leaves are three-dimensional.

▶ *The delicate leaflets of the seed fern* Neuropteris *have been preserved as a carbon film inside an iron-stone nodule.*

◄ *None of the original carbon remains in this specimen of* Eupecopteris, *another seed fern. Nodules have to be opened very carefully to reveal such fossils.*

As well as perfect plants, these rocks contain an amazing variety of other fossils, and geologists can work out the details of the habitats in which they lived.

Marine and fresh-water creatures are found here. Fossils of jellyfish (only preserved in ideal circumstances), worms, amphibians and fish all occur in the Mazon Creek strata.

As often occurs in cases of exceptional fossilization, there are fossils of soft-bodied creatures that are otherwise unknown.

Other examples of nodules containing exceptional fossils are those from the Carboniferous rocks of Lancashire, and the ammonite-bearing nodules of the British Lower Jurassic.

...FASCINATING FACT...

Spiders, scorpions, centipedes and millipedes are fossilized at Mazon Creek, giving us a glimpse into a Carboniferous world that is unknown elsewhere.

Glossopteris and continental drift

- *Glossopteris* is an extinct seed fern. Its fossils occur in the southern landmasses of Antarctica, Australia, New Zealand, South America and southern Africa.

- **This plant** had a treelike appearance and was up to 6 m tall.

- **Usually only** the delicately veined leaves are found as fossils.

- **One of the most famous** geological books is *The Origins of Continents and Oceans*, written by Alfred Wegener, and published in 1924.

- **In this book**, Wegener puts together evidence to prove that the southern continents were at one time joined as a single landmass and have now drifted apart to their present positions.

- **Wegener was not a geologist** but a meteorologist, and his ideas were initially dismissed by the leading geologists of the time.

- **Because** *Glossopteris* occurs in the southern continents, which are now hundreds of miles away from each other, Wegener was able to use it as one of his key pieces of evidence to show that these areas had once been joined.

- **The problem** when he put forward his theory was that it was not understood how the continents could move.

- **Today** we have the knowledge of plate tectonics, which shows how the ocean basins form and how the continents move, proving that Wegener was correct.

▶ Glossopteris *grew to around 6 m in height. It may have grown with a treelike or bushy habit.*

312

▲ *These iron-stained* Glossopteris *leaves are from Australia.*

The theory of plate tectonics shows that the continents move at about 2.3 cm a year, the same speed at which your finger nails grow.

Ginkgo and other living fossils

- **The expression 'living fossil'** is often used to describe a plant or animal that occurs as a fossil in rocks formed many millions of years ago, and also lives today.

- **Living fossils** have been changed very little by evolution and have a very stable habitat and way of life.

- *Ginkgo biloba*, the maidenhair tree, is grown in many countries, including the UK, as an ornamental tree, and is prized for its medicinal properties.

▶ *A leaf from the modern maidenhair tree,* Ginkgo biloba, *is very similar to the Jurassic fossil leaves.*

In China, *Ginkgo* was cultivated in temple gardens as a sacred tree. It was thought to be extinct until some were found in the wild in southeast China in 1956.

Leaves of *Ginkgo*, usually preserved as carbon impressions, have been fossilized in rocks from the Permian Period (290–248 million years ago).

Fossilized *Ginkgo* leaves are virtually the same as those of the living tree.

The leaves of *Ginkgo* are very distinctive, being almost triangular in shape and partly indented.

- **Some of the best** *Ginkgo* fossils are from Jurassic strata on the coast of North Yorkshire, UK.

- **The brachiopod shellfish** *Lingula*, occurs in rocks of Cambrian age (545–495 million years ago). It is one of the earliest examples of a living fossil.

◀ *Leaves of* Ginkgo *from Jurassic strata in North Yorkshire, UK.*

> ...FASCINATING FACT...
> Other well-known living fossils include the coelacanth, a fish thought to have been extinct for more than 60 million years until one was caught off South Africa in 1938.

Mesozoic and Cenozoic plants

- **Many ferns and fernlike plants** are fossilized in rocks formed during the Jurassic Period.

- *Coniopteris* is a fern found in Jurassic rocks. It occurs in North America, Europe and Asia.

▼ *These delicate leaves are from the fernlike Jurassic plant,* Williamsonia, *which flourished in the swamp forests of the middle Jurassic Period.*

...**FASCINATING FACT**...
Flowers provide a way for plants to evolve, as pollen can combine
the genes of one plant with those of another.

Another common Jurassic plant is *Williamsonia*. This is an extinct plant
with fernlike leaves, which are usually preserved as black carbon films
on bedding surfaces. It had cones rather than typical modern flowers.

The evolution of flowering plants began towards the middle of the
Mesozoic Era.

There is evidence that plants with flower-like structures lived early in the
Cretaceous Period (142–65 million years ago), but fossils of true flowers
only occur towards the late Cretaceous.

Much of the evidence that early plants bore flowers comes from
fossil pollen.

Fossil pollen is invaluable in helping to work out changes in the climate
of the past.

The evolution of insects is closely linked to the development of
flowering plants. Insects feed on nectar and pollen, and carry pollen
from flower to flower.

Fossil insects are often perfectly preserved in amber, the hardened resin
from pine and similar trees.

Fossil corals

- **Much limestone**, especially that deposited during the Palaeozoic Era, consists of fossilized corals and coral fragments.

- **The earliest corals** are simple 'tabulate' corals, which first appeared as fossils in rocks of the Ordovician Period.

- **Tabulate corals** have a tubular structure and may be attached to others to form a colony. The tube (corallite) is divided horizontally by sheets of calcite called tabulae.

- **The coral organism**, or polyp, was rather like a small sea anemone, and lived at the top of the tube.

- **Tabulate corals** became extinct in the Permian Period.

- *Dibunophyllum* belongs to a group called the 'rugose' corals. These are more complex than the tabulate group.

In the Silurian and Carboniferous Periods, rugose corals built large, shallow sea reefs, in which numerous fossils of corals, brachiopods, molluscs, crinoids and trilobites are found.

The rugose corals became extinct at a similar time to the tabulate corals, in the Permian Period.

● **Some corals** in the Carboniferous Period are used as zone fossils. Each coral species represents a small part of geological time.

● **Modern corals** began to evolve early in the Mesozoic Era.

◀ *The delicate internal structure of corals is often well preserved in fossils, as seen in this species,* Dibunophyllum.

Lower Palaeozoic corals

- **Tabulate and rugose corals** flourished during the Lower Palaeozoic Era and at times built up large reefs.

- **Corals are easily fossilized**. They are made of calcium carbonate – the mineral calcite – which is stable in limestone. Also, they are solid structures that are not easily eroded or broken.

- **Coral reefs** are good indicators of marine conditions and water depth. Their fossils help to reconstruct the ancient reef habitat.

- **Fossil molluscs**, brachiopods, trilobites, bryozoans and crinoids are also found in rocks formed in these reef habitats.

- *Halysites* is a tabulate coral with a colonial structure. Its common name is chain coral because the individual corallites are linked together in a chain.

- **Lime mud** was easily trapped within the structure of corals such as *Halysites* and so limestone was able to form.

- **Some tabulate corals** grew as large mounds on the shallow seabed. *Favosites* is a colonial coral, with numerous small corallites joined in a honeycomb structure and is commonly known as honeycomb coral.

- **Both *Halysites* and *Favosites*** are common in reef limestones formed during the Silurian Period.

- **These corals** became extinct towards the end of the Devonian Period.

- *Halysites* and *Favosites* occur in many parts of the world including the UK, North America, Asia and Australia, suggesting that shallow marine conditions were widespread.

▶ *A fossil of* Halysites, *a typ of coral. Its chainlike structu is clearly visible.*

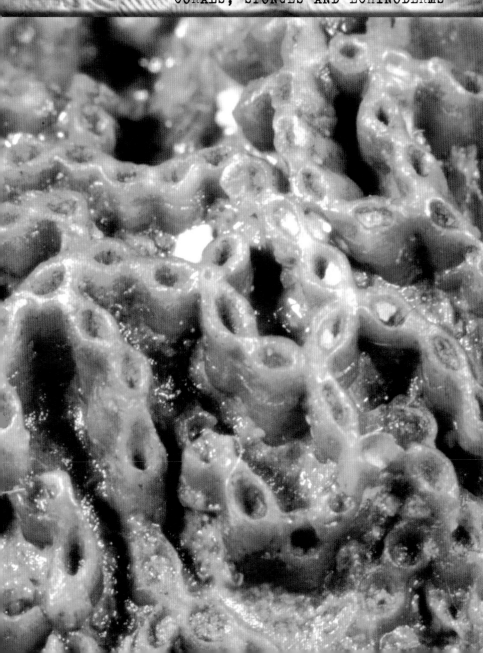

Time recording in the Palaeozoic

- **Fossils can be used** help reconstruct ancient habitats and to work out details about geological tim which can sometime be verified by astronomers.

- **A study** of modern corals shows that they build up layers of calcite at regular times.

- **Within these calcite bands** there are thicker monthly and annual accumulatio of calcite.

◀ *Growth bands in* Ketophyllum *shows that t were probably more than 400 days in the Silurian y*

Fossil corals are often preserved in great detail. This is because the calcite layers of which they are composed are very stable in limestone, and little altered. Many coral reefs are preserved almost as they lived.

A detailed analysis of fossil corals shows considerable differences in the numbers of growth layers from modern corals.

The coral *Ketophyllum*, which is fossilized in rocks of the Silurian Period, has 400 small growth bands between the wide annual markers.

***Lithostrotion*,** a common colonial coral found in Carboniferous rocks, has 398 growth bands per year.

There were, as seen from the coral evidence, 400 days in the year during the Silurian Period, and 398 days in the year during the Carboniferous Period.

The relationship between the Earth and the Sun has been changing through geological time. Corals prove that each day is now longer than in the past.

...FASCINATING FACT...
There are often 360 calcite secretions built up each year on modern corals, suggesting almost daily growth.

Jurassic reefs

- **The corals that evolved** during the Mesozoic Era, in the shallow sea reefs of the Jurassic Period, were different from those of the Palaeozoic Era.

- **Jurassic corals** are classified as Scleractinian corals. They are also called hexacorals, because they have six internal divisions.

- **Scleractinian corals** have many similarities to corals that live in tropical seas today.

- ***Isastrea* is a typical Jurassic coral** that flourished in warm, clear seawater with little mud suspended in it.

- **Modern tropical corals** require similar conditions, if warm, clear water through which sunlight can penetrate.

- ***Isastrea*** grew as a mass of small, joined, individual corallites standing upright on the seabed.

- **When a lot of muddy sediment** was deposited, the coral reefs died out.

- **Lime mud** formed around corals that often derived from broken shells and other fossil debris. This then turned into limestone.

● **Many molluscs** thrived in this reef environment. Ammonite shells are also found in these limestones.

● **Other common fossils** in the reef rocks include brachiopods and burrows made by shrimps.

◀ *This specimen of* Isastrea, *from the Jurassic Period, shows the individual six-sided corallites.*

325

Fossil sponges

- **Sponges are mostly marine animals** that live in various habitats, and can be found today in low-shore rock pools.

- **Sponges are delicate organisms**. They are among the simplest multi-celled creatures.

▶ *This modern tropical vase sponge has a feather star growing on it. Feather stars are closely related to starfish and sea urchins.*

▶ Raphidonema *is a fossil vase sponge common during the Mesozoic Era.*

A sponge is made of a thin, porous structure, which is supported by small spines called spicules. Spicules are sometimes made of silica, a resistant material that may make up certain rock materials such as chert.

Surprisingly, despite their structure, sponges are not uncommon as fossils.

Fossil sponges occur mainly where sediment was deposited in a calm marine environment, with no strong currents.

Rocks as old as the Cambrian Period contain fossil sponges.

Raphidonema is a well-known fossil sponge found in Mesozoic rocks.

Some fossil sponges, including *Siphonia*, have long stems and stand on the seabed. They look like tulips.

Raphidonema has a structure like a porous, crinkled vase. It grew from the seabed, with its wide opening pointing upwards.

Sponges form part of a community of marine creatures. Often there are fossils of bivalve molluscs such as oysters and pectens, and also gastropods and ammonites found with the fossil sponges.

Fossil crinoids

- **Crinoids are strange animals**, which have a plantlike structure. They have roots, a stem and a cup (calyx) at the top, in which the animal lives.

- **Because of their structure**, crinoids are also called 'sea lilies'.

- **The solid parts** of the structure are made of calcite, which means crinoids are easily fossilized. However, it is usually only the stem that is preserved.

- **The stem is composed** of numerous small discs called ossicles. Before and during fossilization, the stem of a crinoid often breaks. Some crinoidal limestone is composed almost entirely of ossicles.

- **Above the calyx** are flexible, feathery arms. These direct water currents containing food towards the animal.

- **Crinoids** are closely related to starfish and sea urchins. All three groups of creatures belong to the phylum Echinodermata.

- *Traumatocrinus*, from the Triassic rocks of the Ghizou Province, of China, shows the flexible stems and calyx with waving arms.

- **Crinoids** first evolved during the Ordovician Period.

- **Not all crinoids live** attached by their roots to the seabed. Some are free-swimming.

- **Today**, crinoids live in all depths of seawater. Some are even found in the deepest abyssal water.

▶ *Each of these specimens of* Traumatocrinus *has a calyx, arms and stem.*

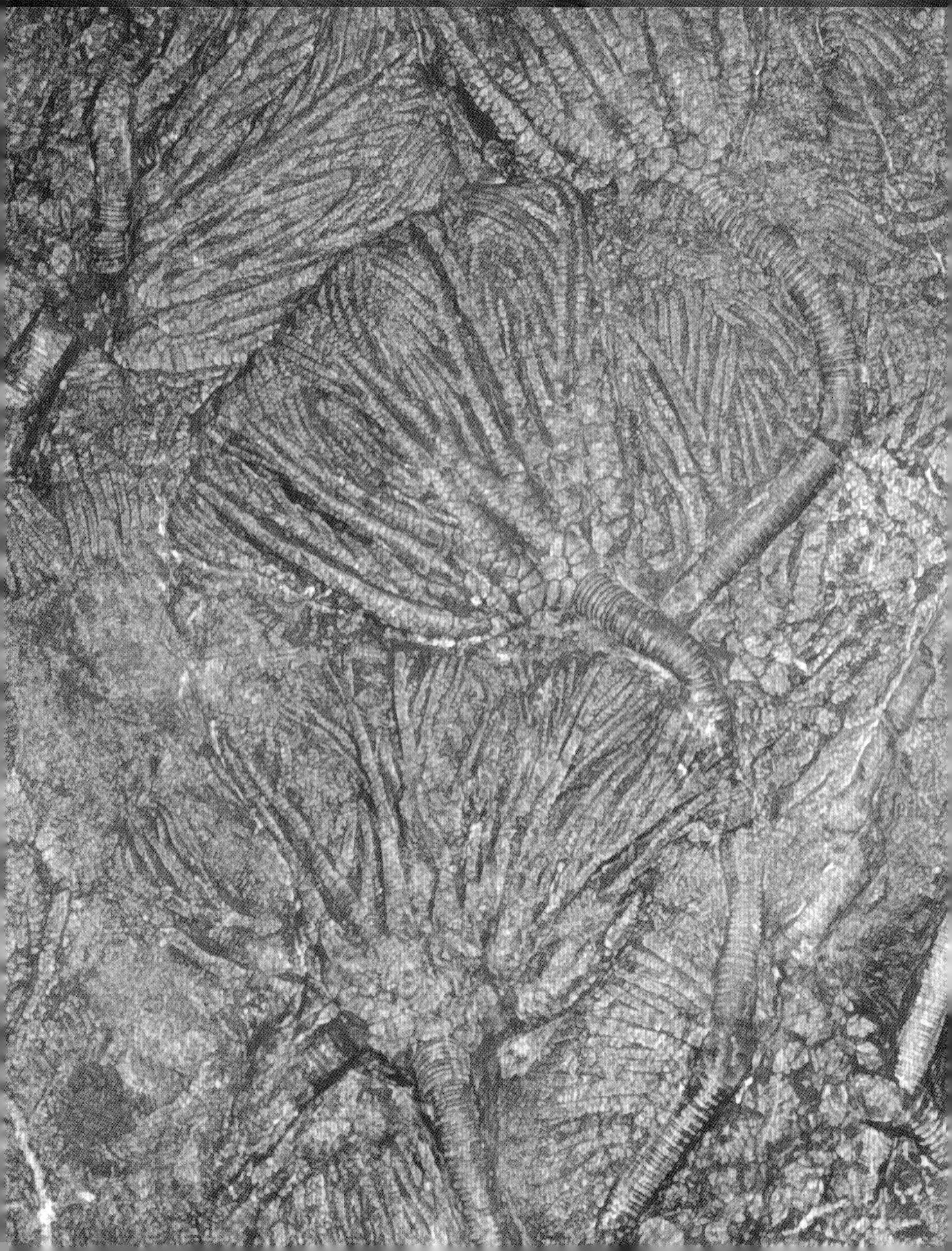

Encrinus and the Triassic of German

- *Encrinus* is one of the best-preserved fossil crinoids. It reveals a lot about crinoids and their way of life.

- **During the Triassic Period**, much of Germany was covered by the sea. This was in great contrast to the dry, desert-like conditions that existed in Britain at that time.

- **Part of this German sea** is called the Muschelkalk. This name refers to the limestone rich in fossil shells, which formed there.

- **Crinoid fossils**, especially Encrinus, are abundant in the Muschelkalk limestones.

- **An important feature** of these fossils is the excellent preservation of the upper structure of the crinoids, the calyx.

- *Encrinus* has a perfect five-fold symmetry, as do many of the members of their phylum.

Calyx made of larger plates

330

Arms made of smaller
interlocking plates

- **Among its close relatives** are starfish and sea urchins.

- **These crinoids** have been studied for hundreds of years, and the name *Encrinus* was first used in the 16th century.

- **By comparing *Encrinus*** with living crinoids, its way of life can be suggested.

- ***Encrinus*** probably lived in flowing sea currents, with its calyx pointing into the current. This allowed food particles to be easily carried towards the animal.

◄ *This typical specimen of* Encrinus *shows the calyx, made of large plates, with the arms, made of smaller interlocking plates, folded tightly above.*

331

Jurassic crinoids

▲ *The slender arms of this specimen of* Pentacrinus
have been preserved in pyrite (fool's gold).

During the Jurassic Period, shallow seas existed at certain times in many areas, including Britain.

The crinoid *Pentacrinus* is found fossilized in the limestones that were formed on this shallow seabed.

Pentacrinus is well-known for the structure of its stem. The small ossicles, of which it is made, are star shaped. Because the stem is very brittle, these small stars are often all that is fossilized of the whole crinoid.

As well as being found in limestones, *Pentacrinus* occurs in the dark mudstones formed in deeper parts of the Jurassic sea.

It has been suggested that *Pentacrinus* may have lived on driftwood and other debris, as well as on the seabed. This could explain how it reached deeper water.

Modern species of *Pentacrinus* are anchored to the seabed when they are young. As they mature, they break away and become free-swimming.

Pentacrinus has very long arms rising above the small calyx. These arms branch many times.

When found fossilized in dark mudstones and shales, *Pentacrinus* is often preserved in iron pyrite. This is an iron sulphide mineral with a glistening golden colour. It is known as 'fool's gold'.

Many other fossils are found in the same strata as *Pentacrinus*. These include various molluscs, brachiopods and other echinoderms.

From a study of the rock in which these fossils are found, and of the fossils themselves, the habitat can be reconstructed.

Brittle stars

- **Brittle stars** are delicate starfish with long, slender arms. Usually there are five arms, giving them typical echinoderm symmetry.

- **As in other starfish**, the animal's mouth is in the central disc. The flexible arms allow the creature to move rapidly over the seabed.

- **Many brittle stars** feed on plankton, but some species eat small shellfish.

- **Fossils** of brittle stars, which are scientifically called ophiuroids, are found in rocks dating as far back as the Ordovician Period.

- **There are a number** of 'starfish beds' in the fossil record, some of the best being found in lower Jurassic rocks.

- **Other numbers** of brittle stars have been found in Devonian rocks in Germany and Silurian strata in Scotland.

- **Today**, brittle stars often live in large numbers in both shallow and deep seas.

- **Because brittle stars are so delicate**, the possibility of them being washed together by sea currents and fossilized as a large number of perfect specimens is remote.

- **For a mass of brittle stars** to be fossilized together, it is likely that a colony was rapidly covered with mud or sand.

- **It has been discovered** that living brittle stars cannot escape from sediment more than 5 cm deep.

▶ *This fossil mass of brittle stars show the central disc an flexible arms, all with five-fold symmetry.*

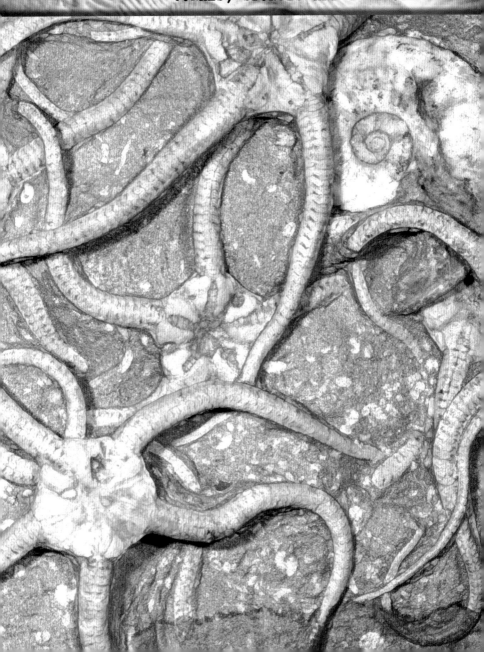

Jurassic sea urchins

- **Sea urchins** (echinoids) have evolved into many forms that are closely related to their habitat.

- **Regular echinoids** generally have a rounded shell (test). The mouthpart is positioned at the bottom of the shell, and the anus is positioned at the top.

- **The shell** is made of five bands of plates, which give it a five-fold symmetry. Spines are attached to the outside of the shell, and thin, delicate tube feet protrude through pores. The spines and tube feet are used for movement.

- **Irregular echinoids** have a similar structure but the shell has a two-fold symmetry.

▲ *This echinoid is called 'pencil urchin' because of the size and shape of its spines. The ball-and-socket joints where they join the shell (test) are clearly seen*

- **Some echinoids** are flattened, like *Clypeus* while others are dome-shaped.

- *Clypeus* is a relatively large fossil sea urchin at about 10 cm in diameter.

- *Clypeus* has petal-shaped bands of plates running around its shell.

- **Modern sand dollars** are flattened echinoids, with similar shells to *Clypeus*. They live on or in the seabed in calm seawater.

- *Clypeus* often occurs in oolitic limestone of Jurassic age. It is often fossilized with molluscs and brachiopods.

◄ Clypeus *is an irregular sea urchin. Its spines were probably removed by sea currents before it was fossilized.*

Spiny sea urchins

- **Sea urchins** use their spines for moving about and as protection from predators.

- **The spines** on sea urchins vary greatly. Some echinoids have a few stout, club-shaped spines and others have a mass of slender, pointed spines.

- *Cidaris* is a fossil sea urchin from rocks of Jurassic to Recent age.

- **On its shell**, *Cidaris* has large, rounded 'bosses' where the spines were attached with a ball and socket joint.

- **Often the shell breaks** up during fossilization, and the large spines are frequently found as individual fossils.

- *Cidaris* **has a rounded shell** with the mouth central below, and is classified as a regular echinoid.

- **In rocks of Jurassic age**, *Cidaris* is found in limestone strata with many other fossils. These include corals, brachiopods, molluscs and bryozoans.

▶ Psammechinus, also known as the green sea urchin, *is a modern sea urchin with many thin, sharp spines.*

- ***Psammechinus*** is a spiny sea urchin that lives today in shallow seas, and can be found in rock pools on the shore at low tide.

- **The spines** on *Psammechinus* are relatively large. They are attached to the outside of the shell in a similar way to those on the fossil *Cidaris*.

- **As with fossil sea urchins**, the spines break off *Psammechinus* when it dies. Empty shells washed up on the shore rarely have spines attached to them.

◀ *Delicate echinoid spines are rarely preserved as fossils. The Jurassic sea urchin* Cidaris *is very similar to the modern-day* Psammechinus.

Burrowing sea urchins

- **Sea urchins** that burrow into the soft sediment on the seabed are often heart-shaped in outline.

- *Micraster* is a common fossil sea urchin. It is found in chalk formed in the Cretaceous Period.

- **Because of its unusual outline,** *Micraster* is classified as an irregular echinoid.

- **Other features** that make it irregular are its very short, petal-shaped rows of plates, and the non-central position of the mouth and anus.

- *Micraster* has been the subject of many scientific studies. An evolutionary sequence of this genus has been worked out.

- **The chalk** in which fossils of *Micraster* are found, was formed as a fine mud on the seabed.

▲ *This specimen of the Cretaceous sea urchin,* Micraster *has the typical heart-shaped outline of a burrowing echinoid.*

Other fossils found with *Micraster* include bivalve molluscs, sponges, corals, brachiopods and fish teeth.

Echinocardium is a modern sea urchin that lives in shallow seas. It burrows into mud and sand.

This recent sea urchin has a heart-shaped shell, very similar to that of *Micraster*.

Though *Echinocardium* is covered with soft spines when alive, dead shells washed up on the shore are usually bare of spines.

▼ Echinocardium *is a common echinoid around the coast of Britain. Its scientific name means 'spiny heart'. It is a burrower, like the fossil* Micraster.

Brachiopods

- **Brachiopods** are marine shellfish that are very different from other shelled animals. They are classified in a phylum of their own and are commonly known as lampshells.

- **A typical brachiopod** has a shell made of two valves. Some brachiopods are able to open and close their shells to let in seawater containing food.

- **The two valves** of a brachiopod shell differ from each other. One valve has a hole in its pointed end through which a tough stalk sticks out. This stalk, called the pedicle, anchors the animal to the seabed.

- **Inarticulate brachiopods** are the most primitive, and were first found fossilized in Ordovician strata.

- *Lingula* is an inarticulate brachiopod, as it can't open and close its shell.

- **This brachiopod** burrows vertically into soft mud on the seabed.

- **Modern-day *Lingula*** can help palaeontologists suggest what habitat this brachiopod lived in before they became fossilized.

- **Primitive brachiopods**, such as *Lingula,* have different shell compositions from other brachiopods. *Lingula*'s shell is made of phosphates and chitin – a similar material to human finger nails.

- *Lingula* is found fossilized in dark shales and mudstones with other brachiopods and bivalve molluscs.

...FASCINATING FACT...
Lingula is called a living fossil because it has remained
virtually unchanged for 500 million years.

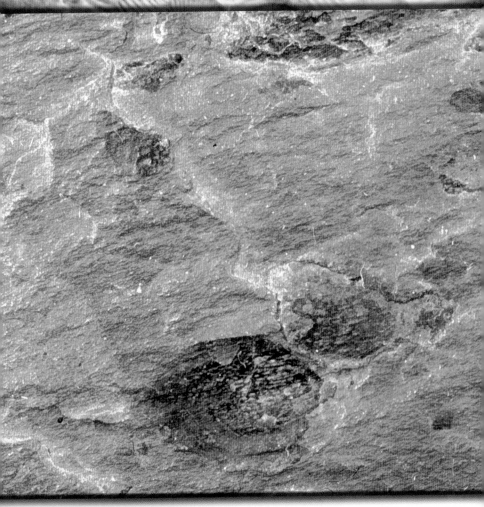

These shells of Lingula *are preserved*
strata of Ordovician age.

Palaeozoic brachiopods

- **Brachiopods** still live today, but they were far more numerous in the past than they are now.

- **During the Carboniferous Period**, many brachiopods, including *Spirifer* and *Productus*, lived in the shallow seas that covered much of Europe and North America.

- ***Spirifer*** **and *Productus*** are called articulate brachiopods because they could open and close their shells.

- **The symmetry** of a brachiopod shell is different to that of a bivalve mollusc. A bivalve has two valves that are similar to each other. A brachiopod's two valves differ from each other.

- ***Spirifer*** has a small shell crossed with thick ridges called ribs. There is straight hinge line along which the shell opens.

- ***Productus*** is a different shape from *Spirifer*. It is more rounded, and some species grew quite large. *Gigantoproductus* commonly grew to 15 cm in width.

▲ *This specimen of* Spirifer, *from Carboniferous limestone shows th straight hinge line and radiating ribs.*

344

The shell of *Productus* is covered with circular growth lines and thin radiating ribs.

Productus often has a spiny shell, though the delicate spines break off easily during fossilization. These spines may have helped to anchor the shell in mud on the seabed.

Both of these brachiopods are commonly found in limestone of the Carboniferous Period.

Other fossils found with *Productus* and *Spirifer* include corals, trilobites and molluscs.

▶ Productus *is a common fossil brachiopod. A few of the spines used to anchor the shell into the mud of the seabed can be seen here.*

Spines _____

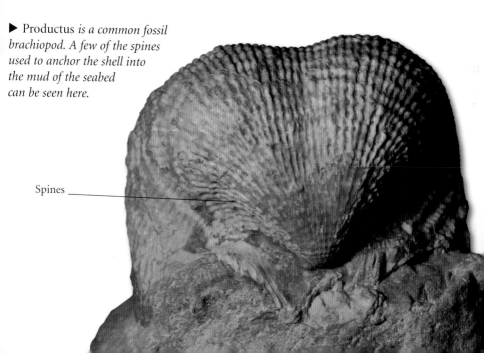

Rhynchonellids

- **Small brachiopods** with heavily ribbed shells are common in many Jurassic strata. These are classified as Rhynchonellids.

- **The shell** of a typical Rhynchonellid is only about 5 cm in diameter.

- **They are articulate brachiopods**, which could open and close their shells. The larger pedicle valve has a hole from which the fleshy pedicle protruded.

- **The shell** is made of calcite, unlike the phosphatic shell of the inarticulate brachiopods.

- **This group** seems to have been very successful, and first evolved during the Ordovician Period. Some species still live today.

- **A notable feature** of the shell is the zig-zag line along which the shell opens.

- **These brachiopods** are found in a number of different Jurassic strata. They are most common in limestones and ironstones, and also occur in sandstones.

KEY

1 Thecosmilia
2 Chlamys
3 Rhynchonellids
4 Rhabdophyllia
5 Bryozoan
6 Cladophyllia conybeari
7 Trochid

- **They are fossilized** with ammonites and other molluscs, crinoids, echinoids, and other types of brachiopods.

- **Rhynchonellids are often** fossilized in small clusters. It is probable that they lived attached in groups to the seabed.

- **From the strata** in which they are fossilized, it can be worked out that these brachiopods preferred clear seawater, without much sand or mud.

▲ *Small Rhynchonellid brachiopods lived attached to the seabed. In this reef habitat, numerous other organisms were common, including corals, molluscs and echinoids.*

Terebratulids

- **Though abundant** in Jurassic strata, the Terebratulid brachiopods have a very long geological history. They are still alive today, and the earliest fossils of them are found in Ordovician strata.

- **A typical Terebratulid** has an oval shell, which is about 2.5 to 5 cm in length.

- **Often the shell is smooth**, without obvious ribs. Growth lines, which show the edge of the shell when it was smaller, can usually be seen.

- **One valve** is bigger than the other. This, the pedicle valve, has a hole for the pedicle.

- **Terebratulids**, like other articulate brachiopods, feed on material suspended in seawater. A current of water enters the shell when it is slightly opened.

- **Inside a brachiopod shell** is a structure called the brachidium. This is sometimes found in fossils. Its purpose was to support the main food-gathering organ, the feathery lophophore.

- **Terebratulid brachiopods** occur in a variety of Jurassic strata. However, they are most common in certain limestones.

- **Oolitic limestone** is a common rock formed in the Jurassic Period. It is made of minute, rounded grains of calcite that form in moving seawater.

- **Unlike the Rhynchonellids**, the Terebratulids occur individually, and seem not to have clustered in masses.

. . . FASCINATING FACT . . .
Fossils found with Terebratulids include ammonites and other
molluscs, corals, echinoids and crinoids.

The pedicle opening can be seen
...his specimen, as a small hole
...d with oolitic limestone.
...e wavy structure on
...brachial valve is
...ssil worm tube.

...dicle opening

Fossil worm tube

Graptolites

- **Graptolites** were simple marine animals that first appeared in the Cambrian Period. They became extinct in the Carboniferous Period.

- **Graptolite** fossils are found in rocks that formed in the deep sea, such as dark mudstones and shales. The name 'graptolite' means 'writing in stone'.

- **A typical graptolite**, such as *Didymograptus*, has a slender, elongated structure, often only 2.5 to 5 cm in length. This is called the stipe.

- **When examined in detail**, a graptolite's stipe has a series of small projections on one or both sides, giving the appearance of the teeth found on a saw. These are called thecae, and in life were small cups in which tiny marine creatures called zooids lived.

- **The graptolite** is the structure built up by a colony of zooids and was either anchored to the seabed, or in other cases, floated on ocean currents.

- **Originally**, graptolites were classified with small colonial marine organisms called hydrozoans. In the 1940s, their classification was reorganized, when their biology was closely examined.

- **Graptolites are classified** in their own phylum, the Hemichordata, which also includes acorn worms and pterobranchs.

- **Because they are so delicate**, graptolites are preserved in only the finest-grained sedimentary rocks. They often occur in great masses, looking like pencil marks on the bedding planes.

- **Sometimes** they are preserved in iron pyrite, and three-dimensional preservation occurs in rare cases.

- *Didymograptus* is found in strata of Ordovician age.

▲ Didymograptus *can be identified by the 'V' shaped position of the two stipes. The saw-tooth thecae are on the inside of the 'V'.*

Graptolites and geological time

- **Though graptolites** are very delicate organisms, they are widespread geographically in certain strata from the Lower Palaeozoic Era.

- **Graptolites evolved** into many different species, and in some rocks are very common fossils.

- **A sequence of strata** has been established using graptolites as relative time markers (zone fossils). *Monograptus* is used as a zone fossil for rocks of the Silurian Period.

- ***Monograptus*** has a single stipe, with thecae only on one side, giving it the appearance of a miniature hack saw.

- **Graptolites** with thecae only on one side of the stipe are called uniserial graptolites. If the thecae are on both sides, they are called biserial graptolites.

- **Graptolites**, such as Monograptus, are believed to have been planktonic, carried by sea currents, while possibly attached to floating material.

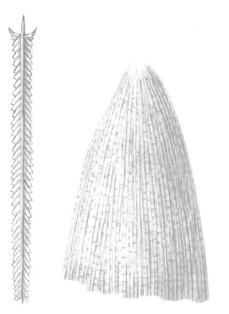

Orthograptus   *Dictyonema*

It is possible that many planktonic graptolites would have drifted into areas where coarse sediment was deposited. Because graptolites are so delicate, they would have been crushed and destroyed as these rocks formed.

In some areas, many thousands of *Monograptus* are fossilized on single bedding planes.

Some of the best-preserved graptolites have been found in Silurian rocks in Germany and Poland. These rocks occur as boulders, slowly carried by glaciers from the bed of the Baltic Sea.

Perfectly preserved graptolites can be removed from these boulders by dissolving pieces of the rock in acid.

Many different types of graptolites evolved. Some had single stipes, like Monograptus, *ers joined together in a colony, like* Dictyonema.

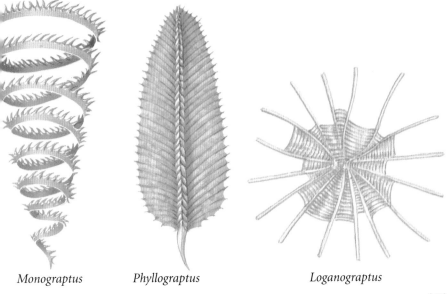

Monograptus   Phyllograptus   Loganograptus

Arthropods

- **Arthropods** are one of the most varied and successful groups of creatures to have evolved.

- **The first arthropods** are found fossilized in rocks of Cambrian age. They are still numerous in all manner of habitats today.

- **The scientific name** for the arthropod group is phylum Arthropoda. It contains creatures that can fly, swim, burrow and sting.

- **Butterflies and moths**, crabs and lobsters, shrimps, centipedes spiders and scorpions are all arthropods.

- **These creatures** have a tough outer skin (exoskeleton), which protects and holds together the soft body.

- **As an arthropod grows**, it sheds its exoskeleton. Many pass through a larval stage, and moult as the larva grows.

- **Some arthropods have claws**, others wings and most have segmented legs and thin, flexible feelers.

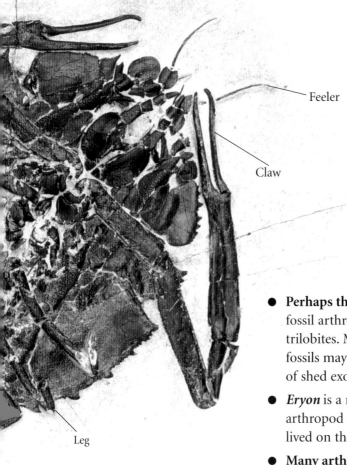

Feeler

Claw

Leg

▲ Eryon *is an arthropod from Jurassic strata. It was an early member of the crab and lobster group, Decapoda. The segmented exoskeleton, legs, feelers and claws have been perfectly preserved.*

- **Perhaps the best-known** fossil arthropods are the trilobites. Many trilobite fossils may be the remains of shed exoskeletons.

- *Eryon* is a marine arthropod that probably lived on the seabed.

- **Many arthropods** have excellent vision. Trilobites were the first known animals complex eyes that could form detailed images.

355

Giant sea scorpions

- **During the Palaeozoic Era**, arthropods called eurypterids (giant sea scorpions) terrorized the seabed.

- **The first eurypterids** appeared in the Ordovician Period, and became extinct in the Permian Period.

- **The largest** eurypterid grew to 2 m in length, however some were just 10 cm long.

- **These arthropods** had a tough outer skeleton, which they moulted as they grew.

▼ Pterygotus, *a giant sea scorpion, had good vision and large claws for grasping prey. At least one pair of limb was adapted for swimming.*

▲ *This fossil sea scorpion,* Baltoeurypterus, *is from Silurian rocks in the Ukraine. It is shown here at life size.*

The body was long and flexible, and had six pairs of limbs. The pair nearest the tail were paddle-shaped, and were probably used for moving through the water.

The head was small, but in some kinds had huge, elongated claws extending from it.

Eurypterids were good swimmers and relied on their long claws to grab prey.

Compound eyes allowed these creatures to detect and catch their prey.

As well as marine eurypterids, many other species also lived in brackish or fresh water.

357

Fossil insects

◄ *This delicate fossilized mayfly is from rocks of Cretaceous age in Brazil. Even the wings have been preserved in the very fine-grained sediment.*

Insects have all the main features of the arthropods. Many of them are also able to fly.

Even though they are delicate, insects have a tough exoskeleton. For this reason, the fossil record of insects is surprisingly good.

Insects often need special circumstances to become fossilized. Very fine-grained, dustlike sediment helps to preserve delicate details.

Many insects have been preserved in amber, the hardened resin that oozes from pine and similar trees. Insects that got stuck in the resin could become perfectly fossilized.

Because many insects live on land, their fossils are less common than sea-dwelling arthropods.

Insects first appeared as fossils in rocks of Devonian age.

During the Carboniferous Period, giant dragonflies flew over the swamps that covered much of Europe and North America.

Some insects pass through various stages of development (metamorphosis). Fossils of caterpillars and chrysalids have been found in rocks of Mesozoic age.

The first insects were probably predators. When flowering plants developed in the Mesozoic Era, they provided pollen and nectar as food for many insects. In turn, insects carried pollen from flower to flower, and helped fertilize plants.

It has been suggested that insect DNA could be recovered from fossils in amber. This is highly unlikely, as the chemical structure of DNA breaks down quickly.

Fossil crabs

- **As with other arthropods**, crabs have a hard outer skeleton, and moult as they grow.

- **The legs**, feelers and claws are attached underneath the body. Here, there is less exoskeleton and the crab may be more vulnerable to attack from predators.

- **Modern-day king crabs** are not crustaceans but chelicerates and are related to spiders and scorpions. They have a structure that is similar to that of the trilobites.

- *Mesolimulus* is a fossil king crab from Jurassic strata in southern Germany. It is very similar to certain modern king crabs.

- **The limestones** at Solnhofen, in which this and other delicate fossils have been preserved, are one of the most famous fossil deposits.

- **Other creatures** fossilized here include jellyfish, worms and arthropods such as shrimps and insects.

- **Mesolimulus** has a long tail spine and curved head shield.

- **Curved compound eyes** are positioned on each side of the head shield, and there are claws at the front.

Liocarcinus is a typically modern fossil crab of the Crustacea group from Pleistocene strata at Rimini, Italy.

This crab had a strong upper exoskeleton, often called the carapace, which allowed it to be preserved in sandstone.

▲ *With a tough carapace, claws and legs, crabs are quite easily fossilized. Here* Liocarcinus *is preserved in Pleistocene sandstone.*

361

Aeger

- **This fossil shrimp** is called *Aeger*. Though it lived in the Jurassic Period, it has many of the features of shrimps that live today.

- **The body was enclosed** in a tough 'shell', or carapace, which was segmented to allow movement.

There are delicate legs, and feelers extending from the head, some of iich were probably used for food gathering.

At the end of the carapace is a bristle-like tail, and at the opposite end is a aklike extension (rostrum) extends from the head.

Shrimps such as *Aeger* belong to the same phylum (large group of broadly nilar organisms) as fossils such as trilobites. Modern crabs and insects are also in this phylum, the Arthropoda.

- **Arthropods are characterized** by an outer, flexible skeleton (exoskeleton) and many appendages or limbs.

  - **The first arthropods** are found in rocks of Cambrian age.

    - **Fossils of delicate creatures** like *Aeger* are not common in the fossil record.

      - **For organisms with no real hard shell** or skeleton to be preserved, very fine-grained sediment is needed.

◀ *Much detail of the exoskeleton of this example of* Aeger *has been preserved in limestone from Solnhofen, southern Germany. Organisms as delicate as jellyfish are fossilized in this rock.*

Giant trilobites

- **Trilobites** are probably the best-known group of fossil arthropods. They ar first found in rocks from the Cambrian Period.

- **Along with many different creatures**, trilobites became extinct during the Permian Period.

- **Trilobites** were advanced marine creatures, with a complex, three-lobed structure. They had a central axis and two lateral lobes, hence the name trilobite, which means three lobes.

- **They had a head shield** (cephalon), which in many types, including *Paradoxides*, had eyes. The central nervous system was probably here. *Paradoxides* had long spines extending back from the edges of the head shield.

- **The exoskeleton** was flexible, and *Paradoxides* was able to move across the seabed, using legs attached underneath.

- *Paradoxides* was a much larger trilobite. Its fossilized remains occur in Cambrian rocks in Europe, North and South America, and north Africa. It used as a zone fossil to date rocks relatively.

- **It is a puzzle** to palaeontologists why creatures as complex and advanced as trilobites have no apparent ancestors. They are present in the Cambrian strata, but not before that.

- **Pre-Cambrian rocks** are often metamorphosed and altered, so any fossils i them would have been destroyed. However, there are marine sedimentary strata of late Pre-Cambrian times without any trace of trilobites in them.

- **Their ancestors** may have been soft-bodied creatures, which could not hav become fossilized. Trilobites probably developed exoskeletons early in the Cambrian Period, and then would have been readily fossilized.

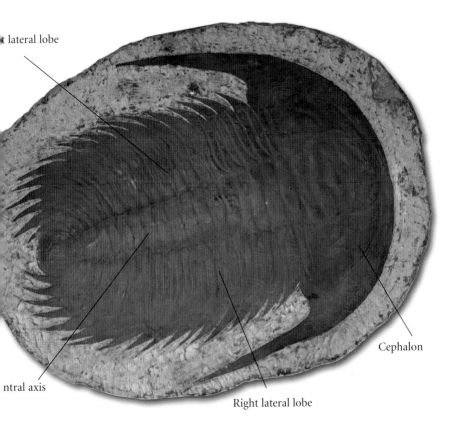

lateral lobe

Cephalon

ntral axis

Right lateral lobe

This specimen of Paradoxides *comes from*
rly Cambrian strata in Morocco.

.....FASCINATING FACT.....
Most trilobites were about 5 cm or less in length. *Paradoxides,*
grew much larger, some giants were up to 60 cm long.

Ogyginus and Trinucleus

▲ *This specimen of* Trinucleus *shows the deep grooves surrounding the head shield. The long spines extending back from the head shield have broken off.*

These two trilobites occur in rocks of Ordovician age. They are well-known from strata of this age in Britain, and also occur elsewhere in Europe.

Ogyginus **is a medium-sized trilobite**. Specimens are typically up to 5 cm in length, however some are more than 10 cm long.

This trilobite is obviously in three parts, with a definite central lobe extending from the thorax to the head shield and tail section.

The exoskeleton has numerous segments running across the structure. These would have allowed the creature to have considerable flexibility.

There are large eyes on the head shield, and short spines, which are often broken off in fossils, extend around the margins of the thorax.

Ogyginus **may have lived** on the seabed, using its eyes to detect moving objects.

Trinucleus **has a very different appearance** from *Ogyginus*, and may have lived in a different habitat.

This is a relatively small trilobite, which grew up to 3 cm in length.

There is a very large head shield with three bulges in it. Around its margin is a fringe with numerous grooves. Detailed studies suggest that they could have been used to sense changes in water pressure.

Complete specimens of *Trinucleus* have long spines extending from the head shield around the thorax.

Silurian trilobite

▼ Trimerus *is a trilobite often found in* *limestone formed from Silurian reef* *deposits. In this rich habitat,* *molluscs, brachiopods and* *corals also thrived.*

During the Silurian Period shallow marine conditions, with reefs, existed at certain times.

These reefs were built up of lime-rich sediment that was bound together by many organisms, including corals and bryozoans. Between the reefs, limestone strata formed.

- **Conditions** at the time were favourable for many different organisms, and these rocks are rich in a variety of fossils. There are brachiopods, corals, molluscs and trilobites.

  - *Trimerus* is an unusual trilobite from Silurian limestone. It has a very smooth carapace (upper exoskeleton), and the three-lobed structure is not easy to see.

    - **The head shield** has a triangular outline, and there are no eyes.

      - **The smooth** exoskeleton and lack of eyes suggest that *Trimerus* may have burrowed into the seabed mud.

      - *Dalmanites* was a small Ordovician and Silurian trilobite, which had eyes raised above the head shield.

      - **Trilobites with raised eyes** may have had good all-round vision. They may also have burrowed into the mud on the seabed, with their eyes protruding.

    - *Dalmanites* has a typical trilobite structure, with three lobes and obvious head, thorax and tail sections.

  - **In some species** of *Dalmanites* the tail section (pygidium) ends in a sharp spine.

369

Trilobite defence

- **The flexible outer skeleton** of many arthropods allows them considerable movement and some can roll up completely.

- *Calymene* is a trilobite from Silurian and Devonian rocks, and has many typical trilobite characteristics.

- **A strange feature** of *Calymene* is the two rounded projections on each side of the glabella (the central part of the head shield).

- **This trilobite** genus has a wide head shield, a typically three-lobed thorax and a small tail section.

- **As well as being found** as usual trilobite fossils, enrolled specimens of *Calymene*, and of other trilobites, have been found.

- **Many arthropods** including woodlice (pillbugs) can be found enrolled, with their hard carapaces protecting the softer parts hidden inside.

- **Like modern arthropods**, trilobites were probably able to enroll their bodies.

This action provides a defence from predators. However, being enrolled probably wouldn't have saved a trilobite from a large predator.

It has been suggested that when they were rolled up, trilobites would be able to save energy if food was not easily obtained.

- **Certain grooves** found on the bedding planes of some sedimentary rocks have been described as trilobite trails. In the USA, specimens of *Calymene* have been found near these grooves.

◄ *Trilobites may have rolled up in self defence. In this position the tough exoskeleton is outermost, protecting the softer body parts.*

371

Butterfly stones

▲ *A winged tail section (pygidium) of* Drepanura. *This limestone is also crowded with fragments of other fossils.*

Many trilobite exoskeletons break up before they are fossilized. This usually happens between the head shield and thorax, and the thorax and pygidium (tail).

Moulted trilobite exoskeletons may account for many of the fossils found. These may have broken as the trilobite wriggled out.

Fossil specimens of *Drepanura* are usually only the tail sections. Only rarely are other parts of the animal found.

These fossils are a very strange shape. They have a central section of small, toothlike spines and two extended spines on the edges.

Rocks containing *Drepanura* often have many broken fragments of other fossils.

Drepanura had eyes on its head shield.

Rocks containing these fossils are often called 'butterfly stones', because of the winged shape of the pygidium.

Drepanura is one of the earliest trilobites to be found in the fossil record, occurring in strata of Cambrian age.

As well as being found in China, *Drepanura* also occurs in Cambrian strata in Europe.

...FASCINATING FACT...
Hundreds of years ago, probably before anyone knew what these strange shapes in the rocks were, they were collected and used by Chinese doctors. The Chinese called them 'Hu-die-shih'.

Very small trilobites

- *Agnostus* is one of the earliest trilobites, occurring in strata of Cambrian ag

- **As well as being a very small trilobite**, about 1 cm long, *Agnostus* has some unusual features.

- **This trilobite** has only two segments making up its thorax. The head shield and tail are both semi-circular.

- *Agnostus* had no eyes on the head shield.

- **In some areas**, great masses of broken exoskeletons of *Agnostus* are preserve as fossils.

- **Some of the most amazing Cambrian fossils** come from the Burgess Shale British Columbia, and from Vastergotland in Sweden. In these areas, masses strange, soft-bodied creatures and large numbers of crustaceans are preserv These give us an idea of what life in the Cambrian sea was really like.

- **The predominance** of fossil trilobites, including *Agnostus*, in Cambrian roc is probably a result of their hard exoskeletons being more easily preserved t the remains of soft-bodied creatures.

- **Fossils of *Agnostus*** have been found rolled up, like woodlice.

- **In well-preserved fossils** from Sweden, *Agnostus* trilobites have been found with an unusual appendage. This has made some palaeontologists wonder if *Agnostus* really is a trilobite.

- *Agnostus* **usually occurs** with fossils of other trilobites, molluscs and graptolites.

▶ *A mass of fragments of* Agnostus *trilobite preserved in limestone. Their typical length was 1 cm.*

Trilobite vision

- **Trilobites first appeared** in the Cambrian Period and unlike many of the creatures of the time, some were able to see.

- **Fossilized eyes** may seem a little strange, as eyes are soft and decay rapidly after death. Trilobites' eyes, however, were made of calcite (calcium carbonate), and could be easily fossilized.

- **Calcite** is a common mineral, which is found in many rocks, especially limestone. Under the right conditions, it can remain for millions of years in the Earth's crust, without being changed.

- **Trilobites** are related to many modern creatures with excellent eyesight such as dragonflies, flies, wasps, bees, crabs and lobsters.

- **Like many modern-day insects**, trilobites had compound eyes.

- **Human eyes** only have one lens, but compound eyes have many lenses all joined together.

- **Compound eyes** are excellent for seeing movement. For example, modern-day dragonflies can see smaller insects flying nearby and suddenly change direction to catch them.

Scientists have tried to work out what a trilobite could see with its compound eyes. Many species probably had very good vision.

Some trilobites had eyes on stalks extending from the head shield. They may have lived on the seabed, with their eyes sticking out of the mud like periscopes.

Not all trilobites had eyes. Some used feelers and grooves in their exoskeleton for detecting the movement of water currents and finding their way about.

◀ Asaphus, *a type of trilobite, had eyes on raised stalks.*

Continental drift and trilobites

- **The theory of continental drift** suggests that the large land masses (continents) are constantly moving. At times during the past they have been joined together, though now many are separate.

- **A number of fossils** have been used to prove this theory, including the trilobite *Olenellus*. It can help to show that Scotland and North America were once joined together.

- **This trilobite** can be found in rocks from the Cambrian Period.

- **During the Cambrian Period**, North America and Scotland were joined. A deep ocean separated this area from Wales, and *Olenellus* was unable to move across it.

- **Although there are many places**, where Cambrian trilobites occur in Britain *Olenellus* is only found in north west Scotland.

- *Olenellus* is also fossilized in Cambrian rocks in North America.

- **The rocks** in which *Olenellus* is found were probably formed in relatively shallow marine conditions. These rocks include limestone and mudstone.

- **The main feature** that distinguishes *Olenellus* from other trilobites is its spines, which extend from the head shield and from the sides of the thorax and tail.

- *Olenellus* had large, curved eyes on the sides of the head shield.

- **It is an example** of an advanced Cambrian creature with no obvious pre-Cambrian ancestors.

A fossilized lenellus trilobite from Cambrian rocks.

Molluscs

- **Molluscs** live today in a great variety of habitats. They are very important fossils, occurring as far back as Cambrian times.

- **Molluscs** can live in both salt and fresh water. Some live on land, and some even climb trees. Fossil molluscs are good indicators of the habitat in which a layer of rock was deposited.

- **The word** 'mollusc' refers to creatures that have a soft, slimy body, which may or may not have a shell around it.

- **Molluscs** include octopuses, slugs and snails, clams and oysters, squids and cuttlefish, and tusk shells.

- **Scientifically**, the phylum Mollusca is divided into smaller groups called classes. Among the main classes are the Gastropoda, Bivalvia and Cephalopoda.

- **Some gastropods** (Gastropoda) can live in water, others on land. They are slugs, snails and limpets. This class is not as common in the fossil record as the other molluscs.

- **Bivalves** (Bivalvia) live in both salt and fresh water. Some bivalves, such as *Mya* (types of clam), burrow into sand and mud. *Pecten* (the scallop) can open and close its valves to swim, and oysters lie on the seabed.

● **The cephalopods** (Cephalopoda) are marine animals. They are amongst the most intelligent invertebrates, with a well-developed nervous system and sensitive eyes. Octopus, squid, cuttlefish and the pearly nautilus are in this class.

● **The ammonites**, one of the best-known groups of fossils, are classified as molluscs, and belong to the class Cephalopoda.

● **Molluscs** are common as fossils, sometimes occurring in such large numbers that they make up most of a sedimentary rock.

◀ *Ammonites are one of the best-known groups of extinct molluscs. They are common in strata of Mesozoic age.*

381

Bivalve molluscs that swim

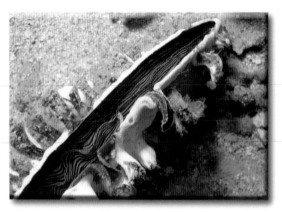

◀ *This image shows the soft body of a scallop shell between the two valves. When the valves open and close, the animal swims in short bursts.*

● **These molluscs** are called bivalves because they have a shell made of two, usually similar, valves, which are a mirror image of each other.

● **Near the rounded** or pointed 'beak' of the shell (the umbo), there is a dark horny, flexible ligament that holds the two valves together.

● **Just below the umbo**, on the insides of the shell, is a series of ridges (teeth) and hollows (sockets). Teeth in one valve fit into sockets in the other valve and, together with the ligament, make a hinge system.

● **Inside the shell**, the animal's body is surrounded by a fleshy membrane called the mantle.

● **Two strong muscles**, the adductor muscles, pull the valves together. When they relax, the valves open slightly.

● **Features** of the many fossil species of bivalves differ, often depending on the habitat in which the creature lived.

These two bivalves open and shut their valves using the large adductor muscle. This causes shellfish to swim in rather jerky movements through the sea.

In fossils and empty modern shells, the point at which the adductor muscle joined the inside of a valve can be seen as a small, rounded indentation. This is the muscle scar.

Pecten has a triangular shell with a pointed umbo. The valves are flat and strengthened with ribs.

This mass of shells is from the early Jurassic. They are very like modern scallops, and probably lived in a similar way, opening and closing their valves to swim.

Fossil oysters

◀ *The wavy structure on this oyster shell is the ed* *of its fleshy body. Oysters have to ope* *their shells so that they can feed.*

- **From the Mesozoic Era** to Recent times, oysters have been common marine shellfish.

- **Some fossil oysters** are very similar to those that live today, but others developed rather different shell shapes.

- **Unlike** most bivalve molluscs, oysters have valves that are not mirror image, of each other. One of the valves is generally larger than the other.

- **Oysters** cannot move freely, and live on the seabed. They have a number of features that help them survive in shallow, turbulent water.

- **Usually** an oyster has very thick, heavy valves. These are adapted to being washed around by currents and tides, without being damaged.

- **The adductor muscle** is large and strong to hold the valves together when the shell is moved about by the sea.

As is typical of oysters, *Gryphaea* had valves that are very different from each other. One valve was large and heavy, the other was thinner and smaller.

The larger valve was hooked at one end and made of many layers of calcite.

This structure probably allowed *Gryphaea* to lie on the seabed, with the heavy valve underneath. If disturbed by water currents, it would come to rest in this position again.

. . . . FASCINATING FACT . . . .

Because of its curved shape, *Gryphaea* is sometimes called the 'devil's toenail'.

Gryphaea is a ʌmon fossil oyster ∘n the Jurassic Period.

Cenozoic bivalve

- **Many** of the marine bivalve molluscs that live today evolved during the Cenozoic Era.

- **Most of the shells** found on the beach are bivalve molluscs. Often the more delicate ones are broken, but some, especially those adapted to live on the seabed, may be washed up undamaged.

- **During fossilization**, especially in shallow water where coarse sediment such as sand is deposited, the strongest shells stand the best chance of being preserved.

- *Venericardia*, a type of clam occurs in Palaeocene and Eocene strata.

- **This bivalve** lived just below the surface of the mud or sand on the seabed, in a very shallow burrow.

- **It had a massive shell**, with strong ribs running across it to help withstand being disturbed and rolled around by sea currents.

- **The wide part** of the shell was in the upper part of the burrow, very near the sediment surface, so that it could feed from the water.

- *Arctica*, a living clam, is similar to *Venericardia*. It has a strong shell adapted to shallow conditions, and lives in a shallow burrow.

- **Although,** *Arctica* still survives today, it is also found fossilized in Eocene strata.

- **These two bivalves** rarely occur on their own as fossils. Usually the strata in which they are found contains many other bivalves, gastropods and fish teeth.

◀ Arctica *is a thick-shelled bivalve found in rocks from the Pliocene Epoch. It still lives today on the continental shelf, burrowing into sand and mud.*

Burrowing bivalve

- **Because** they are protected in their burrows, bivalves that tunnel into the seabed often have delicate shells.

- **Modern-day** bivalves such as *Mya*, clams and razor shells show typical features of burrowing bivalves.

- **Fossils of *Pholadomya*** are commonly found in strata of Jurassic age.

- **The shell** of this bivalve, and that of other burrowers, is often lengthened. The posterior end (the one furthest away from the beak or umbo) is stretched.

- **The modern razor shell** *Solen* is a good example of the lengthened shell. In this bivalve, the shell is virtually a long, flattened tube.

- ***Pholadomya*** is sometimes found fossilized in its burrow, positioned vertically in the strata, with the umbo downwards.

- **As they are confined** in a burrow, these bivalves cannot open and close the valves to feed. The upper end of the shell, the posterior end, is always slight open. This opening is called the gape.

- **Two fleshy tubes** called siphons stick out of the open end of the shell above the seabed. One sucks water and food in, the other blows water and waste out.

- **In fossils**, or shells washed up on the shore, there is often a thin line inside the shell. This is called the pallial line, and marks where the edge of the animal's body joined the shell.

- **Burrowers** have a deep kink in the pallial line where the long siphons stuck out.

◄ *Modern razor shells burrow very rapidly into sand or mud on the seabed. This razor shell has its fleshy 'foot' extending outside the shell.*

Freshwater bivalve

- **Many bivalves** have adapted to living in fresh water. About one-fifth of bivalves living today are found in lakes and rivers.

- **In some cases**, where they are isolated geographically from other similar bivalves, new types have evolved.

- **Bivalves** that live in fresh water are different from their marine relatives.

- **Fresh water** does not hold as many shell-making chemicals as sea water does, so freshwater bivalves tend to have thinner, more delicate shells than marine ones.

- **Many different** freshwater bivalves are found fossilized in rocks of Carboniferous age.

- **During the later part** of the Carboniferous Period, much of Europe and North America was covered with river systems and deltas. Bivalve molluscs flourished in the streams and lakes on the deltas.

390

- *Carbonicola* is a typical inhabitant of Carboniferous waters. It is found fossilized in strata associated with coal beds.

- **This small bivalve** burrowed into the soft mud of streambeds.

  - **Many years ago**, coal miners referred to the layers containing *Carbonicola* and other non-marine bivalves as 'mussel bands'.

    - **Most bivalves** are not much use for the relative dating of rock strata. The bivalves that lived in the Carboniferous rivers and swamps can, however, help to link rocks geographically from place to place.

▲ *This thin-shelled bivalve lived in streams during the Carboniferous Period.*

Fossil gastropods

▲ Straparollus *moved slowly around the seabed, feeding. This specimen is from Carboniferous strata.*

Some gastropods, such as snails and limpets, have shells. Others such as slugs have no external shells.

Gastropods have evolved since the Cambrian Period, when they first appear as fossils.

Fossil gastropods are not as common as fossil bivalves and cephalopods.

There are probably more gastropods alive today than at any time in the past.

Gastropods have adapted to many habitats. Some live in the sea, both crawling on the seabed and floating as plankton. They are also common on dry land.

Poleumita is a typical sea snail from Silurian marine strata.

This gastropod occurs in limestones deposited in shallow water, including those formed on reefs.

Poleumita has a shell that coils in a low spiral. There are ridges and small spines on the shell.

Straparollus lived from the Silurian to Permian Periods. It had a fairly smooth shell and lived in shallow seas.

Gastropods such as these are often found fossilized with many other molluscs, brachiopods and corals. This shows that the habitat on the Palaeozoic seabed was favourable to life.

Cenozoic sea snail

- **During the Cenozoic Era**, gastropods began to develop different groups tha still live today.

- **Fossil gastropods** often have their original shell intact, showing as much detail as a modern shell found on the beach.

- **Though fossils** of *Turritella* first occurred in rocks of Cretaceous age, it evolved into a number of species during the Cenozoic Era.

- *Turritella*, also known as towershell or turretshell, has a long, narrow shell with screwlike coiling. The fossil species are closely related to modern tower screw shells.

- **The coils** of the shell are called whorls. *Turritella* has a groove between each whorl.

- **The only details** on the shell are faint growth lines, which mark an earlier position of the shell opening.

- **Like many gastropods**, *Turritella* lived in shallow seas, and is found fossilized with other molluscs, corals and crustaceans.

- **Masses** of *Turritella* shells sometimes appear together, and make up a high percentage of the rock.

- **Modern species** of *Turritella* usually burrow into the mud and silt on the seabed. The sharp end of the shell points downwards and the opening is near the surface of the seabed.

- **It is probable** that fossil gastropods lived in a similar way. For them to be fossilized in large numbers, they must have been disturbed by sea currents and the shells washed together.

▶ *This mass of perfectly preserved* Turritella *shells is from Eocene strata in France.*

Predatory sea snails

- **During the Cretaceous Period**, gastropod molluscs were not as common as other groups, but in the Cenozoic Era they evolved rapidly.

- **Marine gastropods** developed many ways of feeding. Some became active predators.

- **Almost half** the number of fossilized gastropods found in rocks of Eocene age were predators.

- **These sea snails** were not very big, and many of them had sophisticated ways of killing and eating their prey.

- **Almost anything** living on the seabed would have been attacked by these snails. Sea urchins, molluscs and worms were all eaten. Some species even caught live fish.

Conus, the cone shell was a typical predatory gastropod from the Eocene Epoch.

This small sea snail had a very ornate shell, crossed by sharp ridges and lines. It is often fossilized in large masses.

Gastropods have a radula, which is used for feeding. The radula is a sharp 'tongue' that is used to attack prey or rasp off plant material.

Conus is found fossilized with many other molluscs, fish teeth, echinoids and corals.

...FASCINATING FACT...

Conus has a highly advanced radula that was like a thin harpoon. This was stuck into prey and then venom injected through a groove in the radula.

◀ *This modern cone shell shoots its poisonous radula into a whelk's shell. The venom is very powerful and quickly paralyzes the prey.*

Cephalopods

▲ *These cephalopods (*Orthoceras*) are from Ordovician rocks. They are straight-shelled nautiloids, and the buoyancy chambers can be seen where the shell has broken off.*

- **This class of molluscs** contain some of the most advanced invertebrates to have ever evolved.

- **The pearly nautilus**, octopus, squid and cuttlefish are all cephalopods, as well as many extinct groups such as ammonites and belemnites.

- **Modern cephalopods** have a highly developed nervous system and good eyesight.

- **All these creatures** live in the sea, and most are capable of free movement, often by jet propulsion.

- **As well as** squirting water for propulsion, many cephalopod can emit a cloud of dark, inky liquid, behind which they can hide from predators.

- **Both the external** and interna shells of cephalopods are common as fossils.

Orthoceras is an early, straight-shelled nautilus, from lower Palaeozoic strata. The shell, like that of many cephalopods, is divided into chambers, with the animal living in the largest one at the open end of the shell.

Some species of *Orthoceras* grew to several metres in length, though most were only a few centimetres long.

In some areas, such as the limestone at Maquokota in Illinois, USA, large numbers of *Orthoceras* are found fossilized together.

Specimens of *Orthoceras* limestone containing these fossils are cut and polished for ornamental use.

▼ *The modern octopus is a free-swimming mollusc that lacks an outer shell. It is a very advanced animal, with a complex nervous system and good eyesight.*

Devonian and Carboniferous cephalopods

- **In the upper Palaeozoic Era**, especially during the Devonian and Carboniferous Periods, cephalopods evolved with coiled external shells.

- **The coiled** shell had many chambers. At the wide end of the shell was the body chamber in which the squidlike animal lived.

- **Many smaller** buoyancy chambers extended back from the body chamber to the tightly coiled centre of the shell.

- **These chambers** may have been crushed on bedding planes during fossilization. In many cases however, they are preserved and infilled with crystals of minerals such as calcite.

- **Some cephalopod shells** are similar to a coil of rope, with all the coils (whorls) easily seen. This is called evolute coiling.

- **Shells** where the whorls overlap a great deal are said to have involute coiling.

- **The goniatites** are a group of cephalopods that lived in the Devonian and Carboniferous seas.

Suture line

- **Goniatites** may have been the ancestors of the Mesozoic ammonites and generally had involute shells.

- **The suture lines** have a zig-zag pattern and mark where the walls of the internal buoyancy chambers meet the outer shell.

  - **The common**, free-swimming goniatites are used as zone fossils for marine strata of Devonian and Carboniferous age.

◀ *Goniatites are small cephalopods. The zig-zag suture pattern is clearly seen in this example from the Carboniferous Period.*

401

Modern and Jurassic nautilus

- **The pearly nautilus**, which today lives in the southwestern Pacific Ocean mainly around Australia and Indonesia, is regarded as a 'living fossil'.

- **Fossils** of similar species of nautilus occur in rocks dating back to the early Mesozoic.

- *Nautilus* has a broad shell with involute coiling. The inner whorls are largely hidden by the large outermost whorl.

- *Cenoceras* was a Jurassic nautilus, with many similar features to the modern pearly nautilus.

- **The suture lines** on a nautilus shell are gently curved, not zig-zagged, as in the goniatites, or complex, as in the ammonites.

- **Like many shelled cephalopods**, *Nautilus* has a large body chamber. The squidlike animal has numerous tentacles, eyes, and a funnel for squirting water, providing jet propulsion.

- **The smaller buoyancy chambers** are linked through their centres by a thin tube – the siphuncle. This allows the density of fluid and gas in the chambers to be regulated. The animal can thus control its depth in the sea.

◄ Cenoceras *had a large body chamber, and the inner coils of the shell are covered by the large outermost coil.*

- **The nautilus** has many biological differences from the extinct ammonites. However its shell is similar, and may give a good insight into how ammonites lived.

Because fossilized nautilus shells span such a long period of time, they are little use as zone fossils.

Nautilus shells are found washed ashore in east Africa and Madagascar, many hundreds of miles from where they live. Shells of dead ammonites could probably have drifted across the Mesozoic sea, thus enhancing their use as zone fossils.

The modern nautilus lives in the western Pacific Ocean, especially around stralia. It has good eyesight and moves by squirting out a jet of water.

Ammonites

- **During** the Jurassic and Cretaceous Periods, ammonites evolved into a grea variety of forms.

- **Ammonites** were marine creatures, and many could move freely in the water, though some of the largest may have browsed on the seabed.

- **The ammonite shell** is similar to the nautilus shell, but there are some very important differences.

- **The spiral coiling** of the ammonite shell does not usually extend upwards. It is coiled in a flat plane, with both sides of the shell depressed in the centr

- **An ammonite shell** has a large body chamber at the shell opening. This chamber reaches back for about half a whorl. Usually the animal lived with the body chamber at the lowest point, and the rest of the shell above.

- **The smaller buoyancy chambers** are linked by a thin tube, called the siphuncle. This runs along the outside of each whorl, not in the centre as in the nautilus.

- **The buoyancy chambers** are separated from each other by walls called sept Where these reach the shell, they become very complex. If some of the oute shell is worn away, or removed, these complex patterns are revealed as suture lines.

- **Ammonite shells** can be distinguished from nautilus and goniatite shells by their wavy, frilly or lobed suture lines.

- *Psiloceras* is one of the first ammonites to appear in rocks of Jurassic age. A ammonites are used as zone fossils, it marks the base of the Jurassic Period.

- **This ammonite** has a shell coiled mid-way between involute and evolute, and only faint ridges running across the whorls.

Whorl

Frilly suture lines

Body chamber

▶ *It is
unusual to
find uncrushed
specimens of
Psiloceras. These
examples are from a
boulder washed up on the
shore of North Yorkshire, UK.*

Ammonite variety and movement

◀ *This reconstruction sho
the ammonite* Lytoceras
*swimming in the war
Jurassic ocean.
Ammonites had fo
fewer tentacles th
the nautilus.*

Fossil ammonite shells show a vast range of different shapes, sizes and structures. The movement of different species may have depended on their shape.

Some ammonites were big and round, others were thin and disc-shaped. Some had shells that were quite small, others very large.

The outer surface of a fossil ammonite shell may be covered with ridges (ribs), spines and knobs.

Exactly what function these features had is unknown. Ribs may have added strength to the shell, and spines may have helped protect against predators.

For an animal that was able to swim, various features of the shell could have kept the ammonite in the correct position and helped with streamlining.

Scientists have studied how the nautilus moves in order to try and suggest the swimming ability of ammonites.

Nautilus can move both slowly and in rapid bursts by using the muscles in its large body cavity, and by squirting water from its funnel.

Ammonites had a very different body chamber from that of the nautilus. In the ammonite shell, the part occupied by the animal's body was generally narrow and tube-shaped, though some did have wide body chambers. The nautilus has a wide, expanded body chamber.

It is thought that most ammonites were poor swimmers, especially when compared with modern squids.

By altering the fluids and gas in the buoyancy chambers, ammonites could regulate their density, and were able to change their depth in the water.

Ammonite suture lines

- **One of the most** striking features of fossil ammonites is the pattern of complex lines that can often be seen running across the shell. These are called suture lines.

- **The suture lines** do not occur on the outside of the shell, and must not be confused with the ribs or other external markings.

- **Suture lines** are on the inner surface of the shell. Only slightly worn shells, or shells where some of the outermost material is broken off, show these complex lines.

- **Each suture line** marks where an internal division between two chambers joined the inner surface of the shell.

- **This join** was very complicated, as shown by the pattern of the suture line.

- **Ammonite fossils** often break, and a small fossil may be only the inner whorls of a large ammonite, the body chamber and large outer whorls having been destroyed.

▲ *When polished and the outer lay of shell removed this* Eparietites, *intricate suture li can be clearly see*

● **It is easy** to tell if an ammonite specimen is complete, by looking at the suture lines.

  ● **In a complete ammonite shell**, there are no suture lines for the first half whorl or so. This is where the undivided body chamber is. The suture lines only begin where the buoyancy chambers are.

● **Suture patterns** vary greatly between ammonites. All are very complicated. Some have rounded shapes, some spiky patterns and others are very wavy.

● **Ammonites** are frequently sold as ornaments. Often these are highly polished and the outer shell removed, to show the amazing suture patterns.

◀ *Baculites is an uncoiled ammonite from Cretaceous rocks. The very complex suture lines are typical of this genus.*

409

Spiny ammonites

- **Many ammonites** have sharp, spiny structures on their shells. These frequently break off during or before fossilization.

- **It has been suggested** that sharp spines on the shell helped protect the ammonite from predators.

- **A few ammonite shells** have been discovered with the impressions of jaw marks on them. These may be from a marine reptile, such as a mosasaur.

- **The spines** on ammonite shells are generally very delicate and hollow. They would probably not be much use against a predator, certainly not one the size of a mosasaur.

- **Another theory** is that spines and other structures on the outside of the shell may help with camouflage. The spines break up the shape of the ammonite shell, especially in deeper water, where light penetration is low.

- *Liparoceras* is an ammonite commonly found in rocks of Lower Jurassic age. In life, it had sharp spines on its shell. These are usually broken off in fossils, with only their stumps remaining.

- **On the shell** of *Liparoceras*, the rows of knobs where the spines were can be easily seen. There are also wide ribs running across the shell.

- **As with many ammonites,** the ribs on the shell of *Liparoceras* divide and become more numerous as they run across the back of the shell.

- **Where *Liparoceras* is found,** there is often a smaller ammonite called *Aegoceras*. This looks exactly like the inner whorls of *Liparoceras*.

- **Some palaeontologists** believe that these two ammonites are males and females of the same species.

Base of the spines

. Only the
base of the spines
remain on the shell
of this fossil Liparoceras.
The specimen comes from
early Jurassic strata.

Ammonite names

- **Fossils** are named for many reasons. Often the fossil's name is the Latin version of the name of the person who first found it.

- **Sometimes** a fossil's name is derived from the place where it was first found, or after some special feature it has. The scientific name may tell us something about the fossil's shape.

- **The Jurassic rocks** in North Yorkshire, UK can be easily observed at the coast. These strata have been studied for hundreds of years.

- **Around the town of Whitby** in North Yorkshire, the lower Jurassic rocks form high cliffs below St Hilda's Abbey. These rocks were originally layers of mud on the Jurassic seabed.

- **Many creatures** lived in this Jurassic sea. Fossils of molluscs, fish and reptiles show that the Jurassic sea was full of life.

- **The ammonite** *Hildoceras* is named after St Hilda, who founded the abbey on the cliff tops at Whitby.

- **Ammonites** are associated with Whitby to such an extent that the town's coat of arms contains three of them.

● **Famous geologists** of the 19th century learnt a lot from the strata on the Yorkshire coast. These include William Smith (1769–1839), who pioneered the use of fossils for correlating strata from one place to another.

● **Further south** on this coast, in the town of Scarborough, Smith designed the Rotunda Museum in such a way that fossils could be displayed depending on the distribution, and age of the sedimentary rock they were found in.

◄ *A head has been carved on this ammonite shell to illustrate the myth that ammonites are fossilized snakes.*

. . . **FASCINATING FACT** . . .
It was once believed that ammonites were snakes that had been turned to stone by St Hilda. Local craftsmen used to carve snakes' heads on ammonites to perpetuate the myth.

Dactylioceras

▲ *This example of* Dactylioceras *has much thinner ribs than some specimens. It belongs to the species* Dactylioceras tenuicostatum. *The specific name means 'thin-ribbed'.*

- **This is one of the most** common ammonites in Lower Jurassic strata, and occurs in many parts of the world.

- *Dactylioceras* **has a shell** with evolute coiling. The whorls do not overlap very much, and each whorl can be clearly seen.

414

There are ribs running across each whorl, and these give the impression of radiating from the umbilicus in the centre.

Where the ribs cross the outer surface of the shell, they may split into two. This is called bifurcation.

Several different species of *Dactylioceras* have been described. They differ from one another by their ribs, coiling and other shell features, such as rows of small knobs, called tubercles.

This is a medium-sized ammonite, which grew to about 10 cm in diameter.

As with certain other fossils, *Dactylioceras* is often fossilized in rounded nodules. These are hard masses of rock material that accumulate around the fossil shell. When carefully opened, such nodules can reveal perfect fossils.

In the Lower Jurassic rocks where *Dactylioceras* occurs, there are many marine fossils. These include other molluscs and the remains of sea reptiles, including ichthyosaurs and plesiosaurs.

There is evidence from ammonite shells damaged by teeth marks that they were preyed on by marine reptiles.

. . . FASCINATING FACT . . .
Before the scientific study of fossils began, there were many ideas as to what they were. On the coast of North Yorkshire, ammonites such as *Dactylioceras* were thought to be snakes that had been turned to stone by St Hilda, a local saint.

Giant ammonites

- **Ammonite shells** vary greatly in size. The majority are a few centimetres in diameter, some are much larger.

- **In order to study** ammonite shells and determine the average size of different species, certain rules have to be followed.

- **Before measuring** the size of a fossilized ammonite shell, it is important to make sure it is complete. This is done by examining the shell carefully and looking for the suture lines.

- **A lack of suture lines** near the shell opening shows that the body chamber is present. The shell will be complete if this is the case.

- **Palaeontologists** also have certain ways of telling if an ammonite is a small juvenile.

- **Mature shells** often have widened shell openings and the last few sutures crowd together.

- **One of the largest ammonites** is aptly named *Titanites*. It could grow to about one metre in diameter.

- ***Titanites*** occurs in late Jurassic rocks. It is loosely coiled and has strong ribs crossing the shell.

- **An even larger ammonite** is *Parapuzosia*, from late Cretaceous strata, which grew to 2.5 m in diameter.

- **It is probable** that such large ammonites lived near, or on, the seabed, rather than swimming freely.

▶ *This specimen of* Titanites *is just under one metre in diameter. It is on display in the Geology Department at the University of Keele, Staffordshire, UK.*

Titanites titan S.S. BUCKMAN 1921
UPPER JURASSIC PORTLANDIAN STAGE.
DORSET, ENGLAND.
"TYPE AMMONITES" VOL.III. PLATE CCXXXI
PRESENTED BY H.M. GEOLOGICAL SURVEY

Uncoiled ammonite

- **The classic** ammonite shell is coiled in a flat spiral. Some shells have a large body chamber that overlaps the smaller, inner whorls.

- **During ammonite evolution**, many different shells appeared that initially don't look like ammonites.

- **At many times** during the Jurassic and Cretaceous Periods, some ammonite species developed uncoiled shells.

- **Towards** the end of their evolution, in the late Cretaceous Period, uncoiling was common. Other strange shapes also appeared at this time.

- **One of the strangest** of these is *Didymoceras*, which occurs in the Cretaceous rocks of Colorado, USA.

- **This ammonite** is the corkscrew shape of a ram's horn, coiled in a very open spiral.

- **Many uncoiled ammonites** have a more U-shaped structure, like *Hamites*, from the Cretaceous Period.

- *Spiroceras* is from Jurassic strata. By uncoiling, it has lost the classic ammonite symmetry.

- *Spiroceras* retains some ammonite features, such as the thick ribs that run across the shell.

- **Uncoiled** ammonites were probably poorer swimmers than their coiled relatives. An uncoiled shell would not be as stable, and these ammonites may have moved slowly along the seabed, feeding.

This uncoiled Spiroceras *shell has many ammonite features. There are ribs, and the shell tapers at one end.*

Ammonites as zone fossils

- **Zone fossils** help palaeontologists to put strata into sequences. They also allow strata to be linked, or correlated, from place to place.

- **For a fossil group** to be chosen for this work, it must have certain features. Ammonites are probably the best zone fossils, as they have virtually all the requirements.

- **A relative** time zone should be as short as possible. This allows very precise dating of rocks. It is not much use having a time zone tens of millions of years long. Far too many rocks form in such a huge expanse of time, and correlating them would be too difficult.

- **The ammonite** species chosen as zone fossils represent small parts of geological time.

▲ *This specimen of* Asteroceras, *is complete. Sutures are absent from the last part of the, because this is the undivided body chamber.*

- **Ammonites evolved** very rapidly into many species. Each species lived for a relatively short time before becoming extinct.

- **Because ammonites** lived in the sea and could move about, certain species are found in many different regions. They are useful in correlating strata from place to place.

- **Shells of dead ammonites** could drift on ocean currents, as modern *nautilus* shells do, and be carried to distant places.

- **A zone fossil** should be easily fossilized. A jellyfish may have all the attributes required for correlating rocks, but it is rarely found as a fossil. Ammonite shells are easily preserved.

- **It is important** for a zone fossil to be common. Field geologists need to be able to find them to do their work. Ammonites are numerous in Jurassic and Cretaceous rocks, and these periods are zoned by ammonites.

- **Because** of their varied structures, it is easy to tell one zone ammonite from another, making that part of the geological time scale easy to work out.

◀ *Dozens of* Asteroceras *species are known from many parts of the world during the Jurassic Period.* 'Asteroceras' *means* 'star horn'.

421

Cretaceous ammonites

- **During the Cretaceous Period**, ammonites flourished and many new shell shapes evolved.

- **Some Cretaceous ammonites** were uncoiled, with straight shells. Others were curved, and almost U-shaped.

- *Baculites*, a straight Cretaceous ammonite, is well-known for its remarkable pattern of suture lines.

- **This ammonite** is common in Cretaceous rocks in South Dakota, USA. It grew to a great size, reaching up to 2 m in length.

- *Scaphites* is a partly uncoiled ammonite from the Cretaceous Period.

- **The body chamber** of *Scaphites* is large and uncoiled. An ammonite with this structure was probably not adapted to swimming. It more likely lived on, or near the seabed, with the shell opening slightly upwards.

- *Douvilleiceras* is a Cretaceous ammonite, with the usual ammonite coiling. It had rows of large knobs running around the shell.

- **This ammonite** is widespread and common in Cretaceous rocks, and is used as a zone fossil for this period.

- *Mantelliceras* lived in the Cretaceous sea, on the bed that chalk was being deposited on. It had strong ribs running across its shell.

- **At the end** of the Cretaceous Period, ammonites became extinct. The exact reasons for this are unknown, although they had been declining in numbers of genera for some time. At the same time, many other groups of animals, both on land (for example, the dinosaurs) and in the sea (75 percent of marine plankton) died out.

▲ *This dusty, white specimen of* Douvilleiceras *is found in upper Cretaceous rocks, where chalk is the dominant rock.*

Ammonites with beaks

- **Certain ammonites** have a strange beaklike structure on the front of the shell. This is called a lappet.

- *Kosmoceras* is a small ammonite well-known for this lappet structure.

- **This ammonite** is found in rocks formed during the middle part of Jurassic time. It has ribs running across the shell and spines along the shell margin.

- **In the clay strata** where these ammonite shells occur, they are usually crushed flat, but original shell material is often preserved.

- **Much larger** forms of *Kosmoceras* are found fossilized with the smaller shells.

- **Palaeontologists** studying both these ammonites discovered that changes in their shells occurred at the same time. When a new feature developed on the small shell, the same feature appeared on the larger shell.

- **This side-by-side evolution** of two ammonites, one larger than the other, has been found to occur with other species.

Lappet

▲ *This specimen* Kosmoceras, *with lappet intact, is fr Middle Jurassic str*

- **Palaeontologists** have analyzed hundreds of specimens of *Kosmoceras* in order to try and understand the evolution of the two size forms of the ammonite.

- **It is believed** that the large and small *Kosmoceras* may be males and females of the same species. This would explain their simultaneous evolutionary changes. The sexes of many modern cephalopods have a distinct size difference.

- **The exact purpose** of the lappet on the smaller fossil shell is unknown. Some palaeontologists suggest that the small shell was the male and the lappet was a display device.

425

Fossil squids

- **Squids are cephalopods** with an internal shell. These shells are common fossils in Mesozoic sedimentary strata.

- **The fossilized** internal shells of cephalopods are similar to squid and are called belemnites.

- **Belemnites first appear** as fossils in rocks of the Carboniferous Period, and became extinct just before or early in the Cenozoic Era.

- **The long**, bullet-shaped fossil, varying in length from less than one centimetre to 15 cm or more, is called the guard.

- **As well as the narrow**, tapering part of the shell, there is a much wider, chambered part, called the phragmocone. This fits into the wider end of the guard.

- **Belemnites** are solid objects, made of layers of calcite, so they usually retain their three-dimensional shape when fossilized.

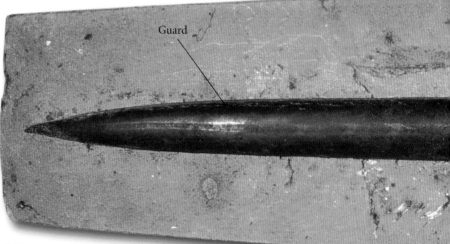

Guard

Where masses of belemnites occur on rock surfaces, they are often all parallel to each other. This suggests that they were moved by seabed currents.

The belemnite's soft body was like that of a typical squid, with tentacles, eyes and a funnel for squirting water or ink.

Belemnites were probably free-swimming, rather like modern squids, although modern squids have not evolved directly from them.

Fossil belemnite ink sacs have been found in Jurassic strata. In the 19th century, palaeontologists reconstituted the 'ink' and used it for writing.

▼ *This is an unusual belemnite fossil, as the crushed phragmocone is preserved with the narrow, tapering guard.*

Phragmocone

Tusk shells

- **Tusk shells** are alive today and are molluscs that belong to a class called the scaphopods. The earliest tusk shells occur in rocks of Ordovician age.

- **A scaphopod shell** is a thin tube that is open at each end.

- **The name** 'tusk shell' describes the way many of these shells curve and taper like an elephant's tusk.

- **Modern** tusk shells give many clues as to how prehistoric species may have lived. Today, tusk shells live in shallow seas, mainly on the continental shelf.

- **The animal burrows** at a shallow angle into the seabed sediment, and pulls itself down using a muscular foot.

- **Its head** is in the deepest part of the burrow. The narrow end of the shell, containing the anus, projects a short distance above the seabed.

- **Using specially adapted tentacles**, the tusk shell feeds on minute organisms living in the mud on the seabed.

▲ *These tusk shells,* Dentalium, *are from strata of the Miocene epoch in Tuscany, Italy.*

Fossil tusk shells are often well preserved. When the creature died, the hollow shell could easily fill with mud. This would prevent it from being crushed.

Dentalium is found in rocks ranging in age from Cretaceous to Recent. It has changed little in many tens of million of years.

...FASCINATING FACT...

Fossil tusk shells have been used by people through the ages for necklaces, nose piercings and as currency for trading.

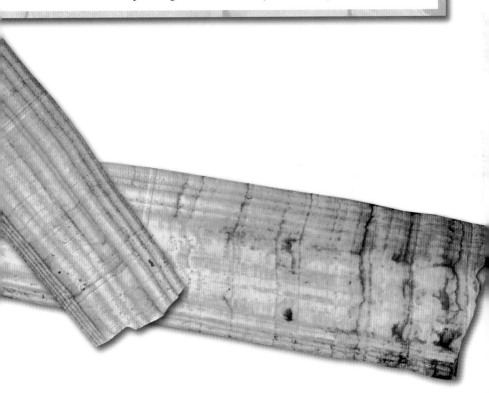

Vertebrate fossil:

- **Vertebrates** are creatures that have internal skeletons usually made of bone or cartilage and incorporating a backbone. They include fish, amphibians, reptiles, birds and mammals.

- **For a number of reasons**, the fossils of vertebrates are not as common as those of shellfish, arthropods, corals and other invertebrates.

▼ Cephalaspis *was an early fossil fish from Devonian strata. Many early fish, including* Cephalaspis, *lived in freshwater lakes.*

Creatures with backbones evolved much later than most invertebrates. While trilobites and brachiopods were being fossilized in the Cambrian and Ordovician periods, there were no vertebrates.

Many vertebrates live on land. Here, erosion and weathering take place, rather than the deposition of sediment such as mud and sand.

The remains of a vertebrate will probably decay and be broken up rather than be covered with fossilizing sediment.

Many vertebrate fossils are broken and scattered bones, rather than whole skeletons.

There are, however, many excellent cases of masses of vertebrates, including dinosaurs, being fossilized in deposits formed on land, such as those in China and North America.

Fish were the first vertebrates to evolve. Because they live in water, many of them are fossilized.

Cephalaspis was a primitive fish from the Devonian Period.

The large head shield of the Cephalaspis had eye sockets on the top, and the mouth was underneath. Like the modern lamprey, it had a sucker-like mouth rather than true jaws.

Early fossil fish

- **Vertebrate evolution** took a great step forward when fish began to survive, even for a short period of time, out of the water.

- **During the Devonian Period**, a vast continent existed comprising what is now Greenland, North America and northwest Europe.

- **The Devonian continent** was dry and mountainous, but there were great inland freshwater lakes teeming with fish.

- **The remains** of many of these fish are preserved in the muddy sandstone that formed on the lakebeds.

▶ Dipterus *is a fossil fish that lived in freshwater lakes during the Devonian Period. It could have possibly survived out of water for some time.*

Fish living in freshwater ponds and lakes are often fossilized in large numbers. If part of the lake system dries up, many fish die at the same time.

Fish scales are very durable and are easily preserved as fossils.

Dipterus was one of the many different fish that lived in Devonian lakes.

Dipterus had a short body with a large head.

Its fins had bony strengthening, which may have been able to support the weight of its body.

Dipterus was very similar to modern lungfish.

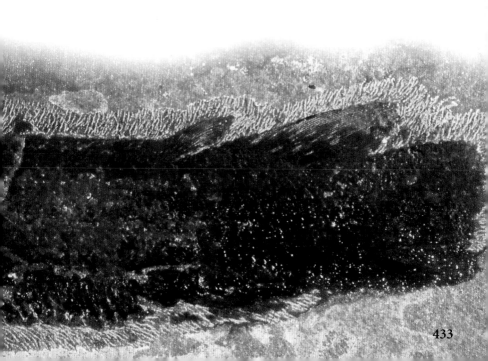

Armoured fish

- *Bothriolepis* comes from the renowned fossil site of Miguasha near Scaumenac Bay in Canada.

- **Fossils** were first discovered at this now famous site in the mid 19th century.

- **The rocks** there contain thousands of exceptionally well-preserved fossils of fish and other organisms.

- **These remarkable** numbers of fine fossils have attracted both professional and amateur collectors.

- **In order** to prevent fossil collectors from ravaging the site, the Miguasha National Park was set up in 1985. In 1999 it became a world heritage site. Any new finds are kept in the museum there.

- **Early fish** were often covered with large scales and protective armour.

- *Bothriolepis* had a large head shield, which is the only part usually fossilized.

- **The head shield** was heavily armoured and covered with rough, bony plates.

- **Extending** from each side of the head were two long, narrow, finlike projections.

- **Palaeontologists** have cut many of the well-preserved fossils from Miguasha into sections. They discovered internal details such as two large sacs leading from the pharynx (throat). These may have been lungs.

◄ *Only the heavily armoured head shield and armlike projections of this* Bothriolepis *has been preserved.*

The Green River fish

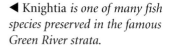

◄ Knightia *is one of many fish species preserved in the famous Green River strata.*

- **Exceptional numbers** of fossil fish are preserved in the Green River strata of Wyoming, Colorado and Utah, USA.

- **These rocks** are limestones formed in the Eocene Epoch.

- **It seems that** during Eocene times, a number of large lakes existed in the Green River region.

- **Fossil pollen** found in the strata shows that dense vegetation grew around the lakes.

- **Many different genera** of fish lived in the Green River area. Fossils of *Knightia, Diplomystus, Gosuitichthys* and *Priscacara* are all common.

- **Small rock slabs** covered with some of these fish are sold in fossil shops.

- **The climate** in the Green River region was probably warm with definite seasons, during the Eocene Epoch.

- **In the drier season**, the lakes became smaller, and many fish died and became fossilized as the lakes dried up.

- *Gosuitichthys* is in many ways a modern fish, with its backbone near the dorsal surface and masses of ribs supporting the body.

- **Many of the Green River** fossil fish are perfectly preserved, but some are in small pieces. This may be because they exploded during decomposition.

◀ *When water in one of the Green River lakes dried up, this mass of* Gosuitichthys *died, and was covered with mud.*

Fossil fish teeth

▼ *This fossil tooth is from an extinct type of* Carcharodon, *which grew far larger than today's great white shark.*

● **Fish teeth** are made of very durable material, and are often the only part of the creature that becomes fossilized.

● **In some strata** formed during the Cenozoic Era, there are large numbers of fossil fish teeth, especially those of sharks.

● **Many sharks** do not have true bony skeletons, and their teeth are all that remain as fossils.

● **By comparing** fossil fish teeth with those of modern fish, it is usually possible to say what the ancient fish were like.

● **Two fossil sharks** that are known mainly from their teeth are *Lamna* and *Odontaspis*.

● **These sharks** were medium-sized predators that grew to about 4 m in length.

● **The genus** *Carcharodon* is one of the best-known fossil sharks. It also includes today's great white shark.

Fossil *Carcharodon* teeth sometimes called *Carcharodon megalodon*, can be as long as 15 cm and occur in Cenozoic strata.

From the large size of the teeth, it seems that this shark may have grown over 15 m in length.

The teeth of *Carcharodon* are triangular in shape, with rows of sharp serrations along their edges.

▲ *The prehistoric shark* Hybodus *was a fierce predator, and had many rows of triangular, backward-facing teeth.*

439

Early amphibians

▼ *This fossil temnospondyl (primitive amphibian) is from Odenheim, Germany. Only an outline of its body remains, with black carbon traces of the skeleton. It resembles today's newts and salamanders.*

- **The earliest fossil amphibians** are found in rocks of Devonian age.

- **The first amphibians** probably evolved from fish, such as lungfish, which are similar to *Dipterus*.

- **Modern amphibians** depend on water for survival. Most lay their eggs in water, and their young live in water before being able to breathe air and live on land.

- **Temnospondyls** are a group of early amphibians. Their fossils occur in Carboniferous and younger rocks.

- **With a bony skeleton** and limbs, temnospondyls share many features with modern amphibians.

Temnospondyls had a flexible body, which was probably well-adapted to moving in damp habitats.

In West Lothian, Scotland, UK, virtually complete temnospondyl skeletons have been found in rock of Carboniferous age.

The late Carboniferous swamps were an ideal habitat for amphibians.

As well as temnospondyl fossils, the Scottish late Carboniferous rocks contain fossils of scorpions, myriapods and spiders. These are mainly land-dwelling creatures.

Reptiles evolved from amphibians during the Carboniferous Period.

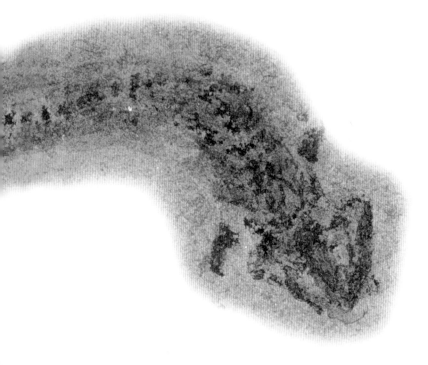

Mosasaurus

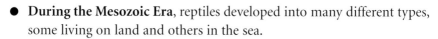

▼ *Mosasaurs were excellent swimmers that hunted for fish and other prey in Mesozoic seas.*

- **During the Mesozoic Era**, reptiles developed into many different types, some living on land and others in the sea.

- **The Mesozoic sea** teemed with life, and giant sea reptiles preyed on fish, molluscs and other invertebrates.

442

Mosasaurus was a very large marine reptile (about 15 metres long) that lived during the Cretaceous Period.

Often only its sharp teeth are fossilized. These are more than 5 cm long. They curve slightly to a sharp point.

Mosasaurus fossils have been found in North America and Northern Europe.

The body of *Mosasaurus* was slender, and it used its powerful tail to propel itself through the water.

A study of *Mosasaurus* skulls has shown that there are many similarities with those of monitor lizards, which live today.

Most mosasaurs probably caught vertebrate prey, including fish. Some had teeth adapted for crushing.

The first *Mosasaurus* remains were found in 1770 in the Netherlands. When first discovered, nobody knew what the giant fossil jaws were.

The name *Mosasaurus* refers to the Meuse region in the Netherlands, where the remains were found.

▶ *These vertebrae and ribs of a fossil mosasaur are from Cretaceous rocks in France.*

443

Pliosaurus and Plesiosaurus

- **The fossilized** bones of *Plesiosaurus* and *Pliosaurus* are not uncommon in Mesozoic strata.

- **The lower Jurassic rocks** at Lyme Regis, Dorset, UK have been a well-known site since the early 19th century. Even today, fossil collectors scour the rocks exposed on the shore.

- **The first** *Plesiosaurus* was found at Lyme Regis by Mary Anning in 1821.

- *Plesiosaurus* grew to around 12 m in length, and its most notable feature was its long neck.

- **The body** of *Plesiosaurus* was short and stout, with four large paddle-shaped limbs.

- *Plesiosaurus* had a small head, and its jaw was filled with many sharp teeth.

- *Plesiosaurus* may have fed by slinging its head at prey using its long, flexible neck.

- *Pliosaurus* was very similar to *Plesiosaurus*, but had a much shorter neck with a large head.

- *Pliosaurus* probably hunted live prey including reptiles, fish and molluscs such as ammonites.

In 1824 Mary Anning sold the first *Plesiosaurus* skeleton to the Duke of Buckingham for £100, a huge sum in those days.

This short-necked pliosaur was an active hunter in the Jurassic seas.

Ichthyosaurus

- **Fossils** of *Ichthyosaurus* have been known since the beginning of the 19th century.

- **These fossil** marine reptiles are found in rocks of Triassic, Jurassic and Cretaceous age.

- *Ichthyosaurus* lacked the long neck of *Plesiosaurus*, and had a long, beaklike snout.

- **The mouth** was filled with conical, grooved teeth, designed for tearing prey apart.

▲ *This ichthyosaur's skeleton shows a strong spine that allowed the body to bend during movement in the water. The large eye sockets indicate good vision.*

The body of *Ichthyosaurus* was streamlined, with a large, pointed dorsal fin and powerful front paddle fins. The rear pair of fins was much smaller.

The tail had bones in only the lower part, and would have probably moved the animal upwards as well as forwards in the water.

Many remarkable fossil ichthyosaurs have been found. Whole skeletons surrounded by a black impression of the body, including details of the paddles and tail, occur in Germany.

● **Fossils have proved** that *Ichthyosaurus* gave birth to live young. At least one adult skeleton has been found with a juvenile skeleton inside it.

● **Cephalopods**, including ammonites, had hooks on their tentacles. One *Ichthyosaurus* stomach contained the hooks from at least 1600 cephalopods.

...FASCINATING FACT...
An *Ichthyosaurus* that died giving birth has been fossilized, with the baby skeleton protruding from the birth canal.

Dinosaurs

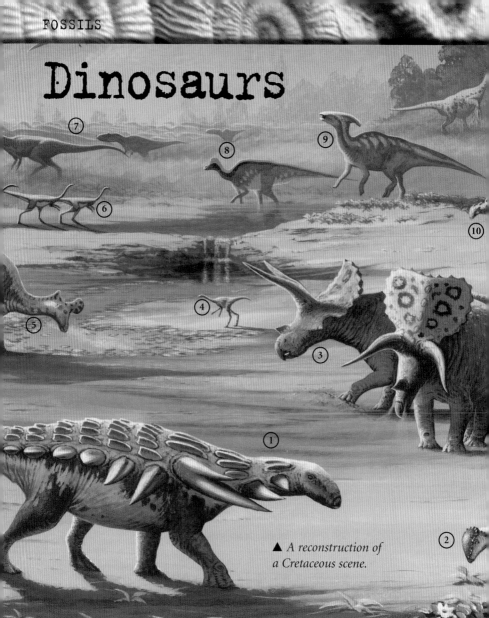

▲ *A reconstruction of a Cretaceous scene.*

The dinosaurs were a group of reptiles that evolved during the Mesozoic Era (248–65 million years ago). The name dinosaur means 'terrible lizard'.

All dinosaurs lived on land. Some may have wandered into freshwater swamps but none lived in the sea.

Dinosaurs are classified in a group of reptiles called the archosaurs.

Other archosaurs include crocodiles and the extinct flying pterosaurs.

Dinosaurs were a very varied and successful group. They lived for around 165 million years, before becoming extinct at the end of the Cretaceous Period.

Some dinosaurs, such as *Diplodocus* were enormous and slow moving. Others, like *Compsognathus*, were small and nimble.

Many dinosaurs laid eggs, from which their young hatched. Dinosaur nests have been found, including those of *Protoceratops* in Mongolia.

● **Dinosaurs** evolved to live in many habitats and to eat different food. *Allosaurus* was a predatory carnivore (meat eater) and *Stegosaurus* was a herbivore (plant eater).

● **There are many** theories about dinosaur extinction. It is probable that a giant meteorite hit the Earth in Mexico, this would have altered the climate and destroyed food chains.

● **Perhaps dinosaurs** are not extinct. If you see a pheasant, note how similar it is to one of the long-tailed, two-legged dinosaurs. Birds are thought to have evolved from dinosaurs, and may simply be modern, feathered versions of the prehistoric reptiles.

Stegosaurus

- *Stegosaurus* lived during the late Jurassic Period (160–145 million years ago)

- **This was** a relatively large dinosaur, with adults growing to about 9 m in length, and possibly weighing up to 2 tonnes.

- **Fossils** of *Stegosaurus* come mainly from the western parts of North America especially Wyoming, Utah and Colorado. Relatives of *Stegosaurus* such as *Kentrosaurus* have been found fossilized in South East Africa and fossils of *Tujiangosaurus* have been found in East Asia.

- *Stegosaurus* was a thick-set dinosaur that walked on all four legs.

- **Along its back**, Stego*saurus* had a double row of large, relatively flat, bony plates.

- **The tail** of *Stegosaurus* was heavy and thick where it joined the body. It tapered rapidly to a point, and at the end it had four large bony spikes.

Brain cavity

Snout

▲ *This fossilized* Stegosaurus *skull shows the narrow snout and very small brain cavity.*

▼ Stegosaurus *had a tiny head in comparison to its body. Its brain was tiny too, indicating a lack of intelligence.*

There are a number of theories as to the function of the bony plates. They may have contained blood vessels, and so adjusted body temperature.

The bony plates could have been held flat against the body as a means of defence, and the tail spikes may have been used to swing at attackers.

Stegosaurus had a very small head. The mouth had tiny serrated teeth. It is possible that food was broken down by stones in its stomach, which the animal swallowed, rather than by its teeth.

Stegosaurus moved slowly, and fed on vegetation. It would probably have been preyed on by carnivores such as *Allosaurus*.

Triceratops

◀ *The horned beak of* Triceratops *was used for tearing food. The teeth, used for chewing, were well back in its cheeks.*

- ***Triceratops*** lived around 70 to 65 million years ago, during the late Cretaceous Period. It was one of the last dinosaurs.

- **The name *Triceratops*** means 'three-horned face'.

- **Most of the fossils** of *Triceratops* have been found in central North America in Montana, North and South Dakota, and Wyoming. Fossils have also been found in Alberta and Saskatchewan in Canada.

- **This dinosaur** was stocky and thick-set. It grew to about 9 m in length, and weighed about 5 tonnes.

- *Triceratops* is easily recognized by its large frilly head shield and three large, forward-facing horns.

- **The shield** around the neck probably helped to control body temperature, a it was supplied with blood vessels.

- **The horns** may have been for defence, or to help with feeding, by pulling tree branches down towards the mouth.

- **With its head down** and long, sharp horns pointing forward, *Triceratops* may have been able to fight off large predators.

- **Walking** on all four legs, it is thought that *Triceratops* lived in herds, wandering through the Cretaceous forests.

Complete skeletons, such as this one from North America, show where the muscles and ther soft tissues were attached, and allow accurate reconstructions of Triceratops.

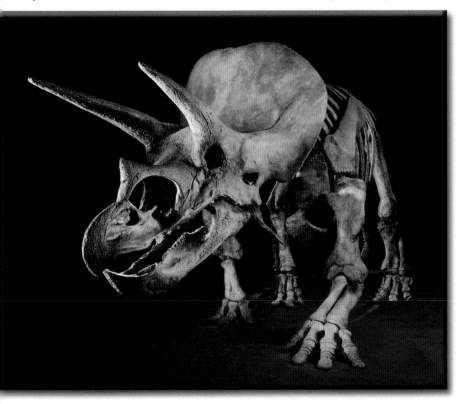

Compsognathus

▼ *The very delicate bone structure, teeth and skull are very well preserved in this specimen of* Compsognathus.

- **Not all dinosaurs** were large. *Compsognathus* grew to only 1.5 m in length. It probably weighed around 3 kg – about the same size as a pet cat.

- **Fossils of *Compsognathus*** have been discovered in France and Germany.

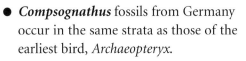

Compsognathus was a fierce predator of small prey such as insects, lizards and perhaps even newly hatched dinosaurs.

- **Compsognathus** fossils from Germany occur in the same strata as those of the earliest bird, *Archaeopteryx*.

- **Compsognathus** lived during the late Jurassic Period, around 150 million years ago.

- **This dinosaur** was slender, with a very long, thin tail and a long neck.

- **The head** was large, and equipped with small, sharp teeth. The large eyes would have helped it to follow fast-moving prey.

- **With long**, thin legs, *Compsognathus* would have been able to run quickly in pursuit of prey such as lizards.

This dinosaur probably fed on smaller vertebrates and on invertebrates such as worms and insects, using its two sharp claws on each hand for gripping.

- *Compsognathus* lived around warm, salty lagoons, in a richly vegetated area. Limestone that formed in the lagoons contains some of the best-preserved fossils ever discovered.

...FASCINATING FACT...

Because the fossils of *Compsognathus* and *Archaeopteryx* are so similar, palaeontologists originally mistook some *Archaeopteryx* fossils for those of *Compsognathus*.

Allosaurus

- *Allosaurus* was a fierce, predatory dinosaur that lived in late Jurassic times about 150 million years ago.

- **This dinosaur** grew to around 11 m in length, and may have weighed up to 2–3 tonnes.

- *Allosaurus* stood on its large back limbs, and used its smaller front pair for grasping prey.

- **The fingers** on the front limbs each had long, sharp, backward-pointing claws.

- **The skull** was large but lightweight. The mouth was filled with curved, serrated teeth, ideal for tearing flesh.

- **The tail** was long and tapering. This would have balanced the weight of *Allosaurus'* neck and body as it stood upright.

- *Allosaurus* fossils have mainly been found in the USA. Some fossils also occur in southern Africa and a similar type in Victoria, Australia.

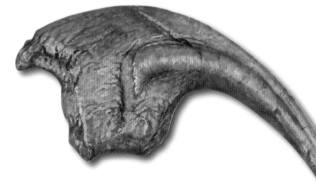

◀ *A fossilized* Allosaurus *claw. The large claws were used to grasp and tear at prey.* Allosaurus *probably ate herbivorous dinosaurs, including giant sauropods.*

▲ Allosaurus *had jaws that could bend slightly to allow them to open extremely wide. Together with its vicious front claws, this made* Allosaurus *a fearful predator.*

● **One of the most spectacular** collections of dinosaur bones ever found was a mass of over 60 *Allosaurus* skeletons. These were discovered at the Cleveland-Lloyd Dinosaur Quarry in Utah, USA.

● **It has been suggested** that these 60 *Allosaurus* had got trapped in a swamp as they attacked giant sauropods feeding there.

● **Herbivorous dinosaurs** were the main prey of *Allosaurus*. The large sauropod dinosaurs such as *Diplodocus* may have lived in herds for safety.

Iguanodon

◀ Iguanodon's *'hands'* *were probably very good at grasping vegetation.*

- **Iguanodon** was a large, herbivorous dinosaur that lived during the early part of the Cretaceous Period (135 million years ago).

- **This dinosaur** grew to around 10 m long, and may have weighed 4 tonnes.

- **Iguanodon** walked on its strong hind legs, and may at times have also moved on all four limbs.

- **The front limbs** were designed for grasping, with long flexible 'fingers'.

- **Fossils** of *Iguanodon* have been found mainly in Europe, in Belgium, Germany and Spain. The first was discovered in Sussex, UK in the 1820s.

- **Iguanodon** was first described by Gideon Mantell, an English medical doctor and fossil collector, in 1825. His wife had earlier found the fossil teeth in a heap of stones by the road.

- **The fossil teeth** were very like those of a modern iguana.
  Mantell therefore named the dinosaur *Iguanodon*.

- **Iguanodon** fed on plant material, which it grasped using its hands. Its teeth, set in a beaklike snout, were for grinding vegetation.

...FASCINATING FACT...

On its 'hand', *Iguanodon* had a large thumb-spike. Early palaeontologists thought this was a horn that fitted on the creature's nose.

Over 30 complete *Iguanodon* skeletons were discovered in a coal mine in Belgium in 1878. It seems that a herd had become trapped in a ravine and had been preserved by sand and mud.

Iguanodon *walked upright, using its heavy tail to balance. It may have sometimes walked on all fours.*

Saurolophus

- *Saurolophus* belongs to a group of dinosaurs classified as the hadrosaurs. They are sometimes called duck-billed dinosaurs.

- **Fossil hadrosaurs** occur mainly in North America, but some have been found in eastern Asia.

- **This group** of dinosaurs lived towards the end of the Cretaceous Period, about 80–70 million years ago.

- **Hadrosaurs** were large, upright-standing dinosaurs, which grew to around 12 m in length.

- **The hind limbs** were strong, for walking, and the front limbs much smaller, for grasping plant material.

- **Plants** were chewed by the many rows of teeth in the animal's cheeks.

- **Hadrosaurs** had unusual skulls, with wide, elongated, beaklike snouts.

On the top of the skull was a bony crest, which in some genera, such as *Parasaurolophus*, extended well beyond the back of the head.

Many suggestions have been made by palaeontologists for the function of the hadrosaur crest. It was linked to the nostrils by hollow passages, and may have been used for air storage, when the animal fed on underwater plants.

- **The hadrosaur's bony crest** may have given it a very good sense of smell. This was important for a creature that was preyed on by carnivores.

◀ *The bony crest was the most distinctive feature of* Parasaurolopus. *Its exact function is not certain, but it was probably linked to the respiratory system, and may have been used to make sounds such as honks and bellows, perhaps at breeding time.*

Tyrannosaurus

- *Tyrannosaurus* is one of the most famous dinosaurs. Its name has become synonymous with fierce predation.

- **This dinosaur** was one of the very last to evolve. It lived towards the end of the Cretaceous Period, around 70–65 million years ago.

- **Fossils** of *Tyrannosaurus* come from Canada (Alberta and Saskatchewan) and the USA (Wyoming, Montana and Colorado).

- **The first** *Tyrannosaurus* **fossils** were discovered in 1902, and for many years only a few skeletons were known. In the last 40 years, many new finds have been made.

- *Tyrannosaurus* was a giant predator, growing to more than 12 m in length and weighing as much as 6.5 tonnes.

- **This huge dinosaur** stood and walked on its massive hind legs. The weight of its body was balanced by its thick tail.

▲ *There is evidence that* Tyrannosaurus, *and certain other dinosaurs, may have had feather-like growths on their scaly skin.*

- **It is thought** that *Tyrannosaurus* could run at around 30 km/h, especially when chasing prey.

- **The teeth** in its huge jaws were up to 18 cm long. They had serrations, which would help tear flesh.

- **The skull** had very strong muscles to provide power to the jaws. It also had flexible areas, which may have helped to cushion collisions when attacking prey.

▼ *The skull of* Tyrannosaurus *was flexible and lightweight. The large, rear-facing teeth are well preserved in this specimen.*

Deinonychus

- **Though small,** *Deinonychus* was one of the fiercest predators, equipped with vicious claws and teeth.

- ***Deinonychus*** lived during the middle of the Cretaceous Period, about 115–105 million years ago.

- **Fossils** of *Deinonychus* have been found in Montana and Wyoming, USA.

- **This dinosaur** grew to about 3 m in length and weighed 60 kg.

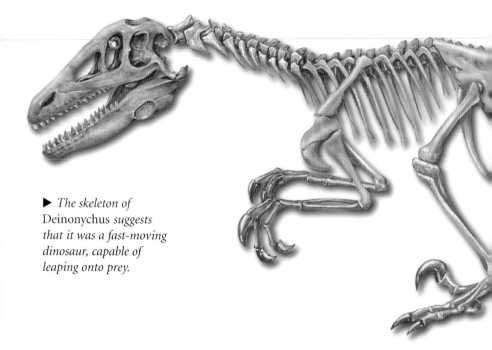

▶ *The skeleton of* Deinonychus *suggests that it was a fast-moving dinosaur, capable of leaping onto prey.*

The skeleton of *Deinonychus* reveals that it was a very active dinosaur. It would have run rapidly, and could probably leap onto large dinosaurs as it attacked them.

The tail was stiffened by bony tendons and strongly interlocking vertebrae.

The elongated head contained rows of backward-facing, saw-edged teeth, and the hind feet had a large, sickle-shaped claw on the second toe.

Because it was a small dinosaur, *Deinonychus* would have fed on small mammals, juvenile dinosaurs and lizards.

A pack of *Deinonychus* hunting together, could have brought down a large dinosaur, jumping on it and slashing it with their claws. The stiff tail would help it balance during such movements.

It has been suggested that *Deinonychus* was warm-blooded. Birds may have evolved from this type of dinosaur.

◀ *Packs of* Deinonychus *may have been able to outrun larger dinosaurs, bring them down and kill them for food.*

Pterodactyls

- **Pterodactyls** belong to a group of flying reptiles called the pterosaurs.

- **Pterosaurs** lived during the Triassic, Jurassic and Cretaceous Periods, at the same time as the dinosaurs.

- **Pterodactyls** are found fossilized in rocks of Jurassic and Cretaceous age.

- **The first fossil** pterosaur was discovered in southern Germany in 1784.

- **At first** this fossil was thought to be of an aquatic creature. Later studies found it to be of extremely light construction, and its very long fourth finger was interpreted as a wing support.

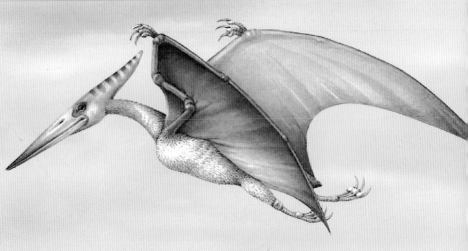

▲ *Pterosaurs like the pterodactyls, could glide but could not fly as efficiently as most birds – their wings were far less flexible.*

The name *Pterodactylus* (wing finger) was given to this German fossil.

The bones of *Pterodactylus* were hollow to minimize the creature's weight – an adaptation for flight.

Pterodactylus had a long beaklike snout and claws at the front corners of its leathery wings.

A detailed study of the brain-cases of some pterodactyl skulls shows that these creatures had large brains, which were in some respects similar to those of birds.

Pterodactylus probably flew in a gliding fashion, and may have swooped down to catch prey.

▼ Pteranodon *was one of the later and larger pterosaurs and lived about 70 million years ago. It swooped over the sea to scoop up fish. Its wingspan was up to 10 m.*

Diplodocus

▶ *Diplodocus had large eyes, but a minute, egg-sized brain.*

- ***Diplodocus*** was a giant herbivore, and it lived at the end of the Jurassic Period, around 150 million years ago.

- **Weighing** around 10–20 tonnes, *Diplodocus* was one of the lighter large quadrupeds. It was, however, the longest of this type of dinosaur, being 27 m in length.

468

Diplodocid fossils have been found in North America, especially in Colorado and Wyoming, USA.

With a large body to support, *Diplodocus* stood on four massive legs. These had hooflike claws, apart from the three inner toes, which had sharper, longer claws.

The thick legs acted like the supports on a suspension bridge, with its backbone in the same position as the roadway between them.

● **The neck** and tail were very long. The tail tapered gradually, and had a whiplike end.

● **A modern** interpretation of the animal's body suggests that the tail did not drag on the ground, as had been previously thought. It was almost certainly held well off the ground.

● **The skull** of *Diplodocus* had large eye-sockets, and nostrils positioned high above the jaws, which had thin teeth set right at the front. The brain-case was tiny, about the size of a hen's egg.

● **Like other giant sauropods**, *Diplodocus* was a herbivore. The teeth did no more than tear off leaves. In the stomach these were broken up by gastroliths (swallowed stones).

...FASCINATING FACT...
Diplodocus's nostrils were so high up on its skull that experts once thought it had a trunk like an elephant's.

Footprints and dinosaur movement

- **As a dinosaur moved**, it left footprints in sand or mud, just as a modern animal does. If sediment washed into the footprint impression, a trace fossil could be formed.

- **Different footprints** can be made by the same dinosaur, depending on how wet the mud is, and how fast the animal is moving.

- **As well as** individual footprints being common in certain places, there are many famous dinosaur trackways.

- **Dinosaur** trackways are found at the Paluxy River in Texas, USA, at Peace River Canyon, in Canada, and in the UK at Swanage in Dorset and near Scarborough in North Yorkshire.

- **In Queensland**, Australia, there is evidence of a dinosaur stampede, with the tracks of over 130 different dinosaurs.

- **Both the size and speed** of a dinosaur can be calculated from its footprints.

- **By studying** modern animals and their movement, a formula has been worked out that relates to an animal's length of stride, body weight and speed.

- **The trackway** at the Paluxy River in Texas shows adult sauropods moving at 3.6 km/h and smaller ones, possibly the young, walking at 4 km/h.

- **The dinosaur** stampede in Queensland, Australia, suggests dinosaurs running at 13 to 15 km/h, and a giant carnivore walking at 8 km/h.

◀ *These footprints were left by a* Tyrannosaurus. *The method of working out the animal's size, based on its footprints, can be backed up by evidence from fossil skeletons.*

···FASCINATING FACT···
Using a formula based on modern animals, it has been estimated that the fastest dinosaurs may have been able to run at speeds of 50 km/h.

Dinosaur eggs and nests

- **Fossils** of dinosaur eggs are not uncommon, proving that dinosaur young hatched from eggs with hard shells.

- **A hard-shelled egg** is a great evolutionary step forward from the soft eggs that amphibians and fish lay in water.

Hadrosaur egg

▶ *Both these dinosaur eggs are from late Cretaceous rocks in Henan Province, China.*

472

Segnosaurus egg

- **By laying** hard-shelled eggs, which were fertilized inside the mother, dinosaurs and birds no longer relied on a watery habitat.

- **Some scientists** believe that certain dinosaurs made nests of earth or mud and nested in colonies.

- **One of the earliest** discoveries of dinosaur nests was in the Gobi Desert in 1922.

- **It is difficult** to know how long a dinosaur egg took to hatch. It would depend on the surrounding temperature, and may have been many weeks.

- **Fossils** of *Protoceratops'* eggs show them laid in a circle, in a hollow scooped in the earth.

- **Maiasaura** was a hadrosaur (duck-billed dinosaur) found fossilized in late Cretaceous rocks in Montana, USA.

- **From fossil evidence**, it seems that *Maiasaura* lived in large herds. They may have migrated seasonally and probably bred in colonies.

- **Fossils** of *Maiasaura* nests with eggs and young have been discovered in Montana, USA.

Archaeopteryx

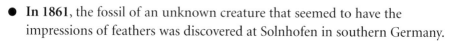

▼ *With a covering of feathers,* Archaeopteryx *is the earliest really birdlike creature in the fossil record.*

- **In 1861,** the fossil of an unknown creature that seemed to have the impressions of feathers was discovered at Solnhofen in southern Germany.

- **The fossils** from Solnhofen are called *Archaeopteryx*, which means 'ancient wing'.

- **This has proved** to be one of the most important fossils, as it is the earliest known bird.

- **The late Jurassic** limestone at Solnhofen is famous for its detailed preservation of very delicate organisms.

Archaeopteryx has many features similar to those of small dinosaurs. Its jaws, for example, have rows of small teeth.

The reptilian tail is also long and bony, and there are claws on its wing-supporting arms.

The presence of feathers, and the large eyes and brain, are all true bird features.

The bones in the *Archaeopteryx* skeleton are not as lightweight as those of modern birds.

It is probable that *Archaeopteryx* could glide rather than fly efficiently.

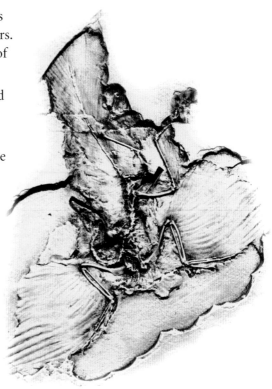

▶ Archaeopteryx *feathers were proper flight feathers and were not just used for keeping warm.*

...FASCINATING FACT...
Only seven *Archaeopteryx* fossils have been found. Two had previously been catalogued as small dinosaurs.

The first mammals

- **Mammals** differ from reptiles in a number of important ways. They have fur, are warm-blooded, and feed their young with milk. Also, the great majority of mammals give birth to live young.

- **The first mammals** are found fossilized in rocks from the Triassic Period (248–206 million years ago).

- **Near Bristol, UK**, is a famous site for early mammal fossils. Here, deposits containing mammal remains from a Triassic cave floor were washed into a crack in the underlying Carboniferous limestone.

- **The early mammals** that lived at the same time as dinosaurs may have been at least partly nocturnal. Their skulls have large eye sockets, suggesting good vision.

- **In Jurassic rock** in South Africa are the remains of *Megazostrodon*, one of the best-documented early mammals.

- *Megazostrodon* had a shrewlike body and a long snout filled with sharp teeth.

- **It is thought that** *Megazostrodon* hunted at night for invertebrate prey such as insects.

- **Another early mammal** was *Morganucodon*. This rodent-like creature had very large eye sockets in its tiny skull, and may also have been nocturnal.

- **The brain-case** suggests good hearing as well as good vision. Palaeontologists studying the jaws of *Morganucodon* believe that, like some modern mammals, it may have had two sets of teeth during its life, and was possibly fed on milk when very young.

...FASCINATING FACT...
Early mammal fossils were discovered in Jurassic rocks
in Oxfordshire as long ago as 1764. Their importance
was not realized for nearly 100 years.

▼ Megazostrodon *is one of the earliest*
mammals, and its fossils have been found
in rocks of Jurassic age.

Megatherium

- **After their development** through the Mesozoic Era, many giant forms of mammals evolved in the Cenozoic.

- **Tree sloths** evolved during the Eocene Epoch (56–34 million years ago).

- *Megatherium* was a a close relation to the sloths and grew to over 6 m tall. It first appeared about 6 million years ago.

- **Fossil remains** of *Megatherium* have been found in both North and South America, mainly from cave deposits.

- **Much is known** about *Megatherium*, as it only became extinct around 12,000 years ago.

- **As well as bones**, some soft tissue and hair have been found.

- **There are stories** in Argentina that these giant sloths only died out a few hundred years ago, persecuted by humans.

- *Megatherium* had a thick tail and massive hind legs to support it when it stood upright.

- **The snout** was extended forward and it had no front teeth. The animal probably grasped tree branches with its strong front limbs and pulled off the leaves.

...**FASCINATING FACT**...
Large quantities of *Megatherium* dung are common in some caves in Argentina. One such deposit caught fire and burned for six months!

◀ Megatherium, *used its considerable height to feed from trees. Few other mammals could compete with this feeding strategy.*

Paraceratherium

▶ Paraceratherium, *the largest land mammal ever, had strong legs and may have been able to run quite fast.*

Fossilized remains of *Paraceratherium* (formely known as either *Baluchitherium* or *Indricotherium*) have been found in Asia and Europe.

Paraceratherium is classified as a perissodactyl.

These mammals are characterized by having odd numbers of toes on their hoofs. Animals with hoofs are called ungulates.

Only about 19 or 20 species of perissodactyls live today. Their even-toed ungulate cousins, the artiodactyls, have between 220–230 species living today.

Paraceratherium lived during the Oligocene Epoch (34–23 million years ago).

This mammal was a giant, hornless rhinoceros, with a long neck, and massive legs that supported its huge body.

The head of *Paraceratherium* was relatively small, and, in the males, slightly dome-shaped.

Reaching 5.4 m in height at its shoulder, *Paraceratherium* was the largest known land mammal ever.

This enormous mammal could easily reach the tops of quite tall trees to browse on leaves.

...FASCINATING FACT...

At 20 tonnes, *Paraceratherium* weighed as much as four large elephants. It may have lived in small groups like modern rhinoceroses.

Giant whales

▶ *The prehistoric whale* Basilosaurus, *which means 'king of the lizards,' was so named because the first person to examine its remains thought it was a gigantic plesiosaur – a prehistoric marine reptile.*

- **Mammals** took to the sea early during the Eocene Epoch, about 50 million years ago.

- **Most marine mammals** belong to the biological order Cetacea, which includes the whales, dolphins and porpoises.

- **One of the oldest fossil whale**, *Pakicetus,* comes from Eocene rocks in Pakistan.

- **Fossils** of the giant Eocene whale, *Basilosaurus,* were first discovered in the 1830s.

- *Basilosaurus* grew to over 20 m in length. Its body was slim, and the head, with rows of large triangular teeth, was rather small. Modern whales have large heads.

Instead of a blow-hole like modern whales, *Basilosaurus* had nostrils.

The body would have been able to flex in the water to provide power for swimming and the broad front flippers acted as rudders.

The rear limbs were virtually non-existent. They were simply small bony structures within the body.

In 1990, new fossils of *Basilosaurus* were found, which showed that the insignificant internal rear limbs had all the bones of fully formed legs.

The largest known animal to have ever lived, the modern blue whale, grows to 30 m in length.

Ice Age monsters

- **The last** great Ice Age began around 2 million years ago. There have been some dramatic climate changes during this time.

- **Some mammals** grew to a great size during the Ice Age. Perhaps the best known is the woolly mammoth.

- **A fully grown** adult mammoth stood 2.8 m tall at the shoulder.

- **The mammoth's skin** was well insulated, with a thick coat of hair.

- **One function** of the mammoth's huge tusks may have been to sweep snow away from the tundra vegetation on which it fed.

- **The remains** of mammoths have been found in Europe, Asia and North America.

▲ *Woolly mammoths (1), musk ox (2) and giant elk (3) wander across the frozen tundra in search of vegetation to feed on.*

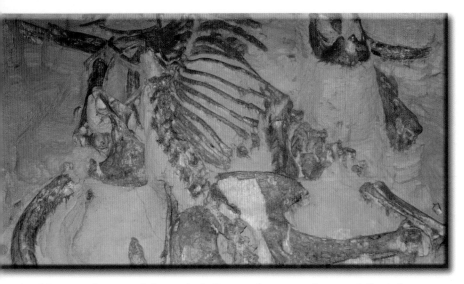

▲ *This mass of mammoth bones, including an almost complete set of ribs, is from Siberia, where it was found in frozen earth.*

- **Literally** tonnes of tusks and bones of woolly mammoths have been found.

- **Finds of mammoth tusks** have, in the past, been plundered for their ivory.

- **Our human ancestors** would have hunted mammoths for food. These elephants only became extinct about 10,000 years ago.

...FASCINATING FACT...
Mammoths fossilized in the tundra deep-freeze of Siberia
have flesh preserved well enough to be eaten.

Hominid fossils

- **Hominids** are mammals that belong to our 'human' group. These creatures are different from apes and other primates, because most probably walked upright on their hind legs.

- **There are many** different hominid fossils from various parts of the world, and it is not easy to work out a complete family tree.

- **The earliest** hominid fossils may be of a creature called *Ardipithecus* from Ethiopia.

- **An important group** of early hominids are the Australopithicenes. These upright-walking creatures lived in east and southern Africa between three and a half million and two million years ago.

- **Working in Chad**, in central Africa, a team of French palaeontologists found a hominid-like skull in 2002, which may be seven million years old. This may be a link between apes and hominids.

- **The earliest** fossils belonging to our genus, *Homo*, are the remains of *Homo habilis* from the world-famous Olduvai Gorge in Tanzania.

- **Many** other species of *Homo* have been discovered. Around two million years ago, *Homo ergaster* lived in Kenya.

- *Homo erectus* lived at the same time as *Homo ergaster* but in Europe and Asia. It became extinct only 50,000 years ago. *Homo erectus* could use fire.

- **Our own species** *Homo sapiens,* began less than 200,000 years ago in Africa. Fossils trace its spread around the world.

- **Fossils** of *Homo neanderthalensis* have been found in many parts of Europe and Asia. These hominids were highly organized, and died out around 29,000 years ago.

► *This skull of Homo habilis is flattened without a forehead. Its brain case is much smaller than ours.*

Index

Entries in **bold** refer to
main subject entries.
Entries in *italics* refer
to illustrations.

507

Acknowledgements

All artworks are from Miles Kelly Artwork Bank

The publishers would like to thank the following picture sources
whose photographs appear in this book:

Cover © L@gui/Fotolia.com
Page 296 Michael Siller/Fotolia.com
Page 399 Christian13/Fotolia.com
Page 403 Bradford Lumley/Fotolia.com
Page 453 Louie Psihoyos/CORBIS
Page 445 Johnathon Blair/CORBIS

Photographs from the following pages are from the
Miles Kelly Archives:

Pages 18, 54, 57, 64, 67, 73, 76, 110, 122, 130, 139, 145, 167, 171,
199, 241, 243, 263, 280, 281, 299, 326, 336, 205, 258

Castrol, CMCD, Corbis, Corel, DigitalSTOCK, digitalvision,
Flat Earth, Hemera, ILN, John Foxx, PhotoAlto, PhotoDisc,
PhotoEssentials, PhotoPro, Stockbyte

All other photographs courtesy of
Chris and Helen Pellant